OSIRIS CABRAL

THE ORGANIC SOLUTION

YOUR WORLD YOUR POWER

Author: Osiris Cabral

Cover: Sabrina Cabral

TO CYNTHIA AND OUR CHILDREN

THANKS

FOR THE LOVE OF GOD

AND

FOR THE LOVE OF MY EARTHLY PARENTS

DEDICATED

TO THE WORLD THAT I NEED AND LOVE

CONTENT

CONCLUSION

INTRODUCTION

Humanity longs for knowledge of its origin and purpose. History only allows us to speculate. At some point, probably only on an individual basis, the veil will be taken down and we will gradually be very knowledgeable of our human beginnings.

Our purpose in physical life is crystal clear. We are to grow in wisdom, happiness and material wealth. Wisdom comes with living, happiness from love and material wealth from choice.

The longer you live, the wiser you'll be. The more you love the happier you'll remain, and the better you choose the wealthier you'll become.

Wisdom, happiness and material wealth derive, respectively, from living, loving and making good choices; live longer, love more and choose better.

The Organic Solution is a formula for making wealth accessible; inspired to end hunger, homelessness, health care aberrations and ignorance. Everybody has come in contact with someone suffering from these calamities. Countries big and small have one or more of these issues unresolved. Let's be wise and happy in choosing correctly.

Governments that implement The Organic Solution will immediately eradicate poverty. Their nationals will no longer seek to satisfy their basic needs through illegal immigration. The prosperous will see their wealth multiply.

CHAPTER ONE

AN HISTORICAL SPECULATION

Fortunately some remains of certain bygone cultures are still standing which speak to how human of those far gone days were physically and mentally built. The Machu Picchu in Peru and the Tikal in Guatemala are very impressive monuments. The sight of the ancient skyscrapers and the technology employed in erecting them raise questions of the physical constitution of that population and how we have come to look as we do today. They were without big cranes and heavy equipment for building and transporting the massive stones put together to construct the pyramids. One must speculate, how it was possible to occur.

Many may remember reading an illustrated bible, maybe as far back as the fifth grade, those that now are in their fifties and beyond. The Egyptians were depicted rather short and not formidably framed. Those stones had to be set in position with the help of innumerable oxen and extraordinary manpower.

How did they lift the heavy rocks to the lofty height that they are positioned in?

The physical structure of the men employed in such tasks had to be gigantic and rough. Let the imagination fly as to the stature and thickness of that people. The average size of the individuals in our population, taken from any ethnicity, is not in the least comparable to how big and strong those men and women needed to be in order to perform the job of building those monuments.

That gives us an example that as science has evolved to constructing bigger and stronger machinery the size of people has been adapting to that which we encounter in our day. The tallest we see are the basketball players and the strongest are the bodybuilders. None of our strongest and hugest athletes have the muscles and tallness to perform in comparison.

A certain race of humans cancels out a previous one according to the need of the epoch. Not cancelling out in an annihilation sense but in physical genetic adaptation to the times. Each generation recording in its memory banks, the human soul, The DNA needs of the next generation and thus making life on earth wonderful and exciting.

It remains evident that every age has gathered the means to undertake whatever project its people has considered; immaterially of the wingspan of its aim. Recent generations make use of mechanical engineering and similar sciences to finish its construction projects; earlier generations we can only speculate upon. Something worth looking back to, as if in a Broadway Theater, sitting in front of closed curtains waiting for the next show of the past to begin.

The relay is a race that requires teamwork. The torch is the memory bank that accumulates all past human experiences. Experiences allowing newer generations to subconsciously pick and choose from old and reconfigure the new. But science doesn't know, or hasn't proven anything pertaining to the soul of humanity, so for the time being we will continue to speculate on the logic of these earthly matters.

According to the theory we present of the powerful race that assembled the pyramids, the Samson people that put together the Mayan Temples, existed prior to the technology we see in our world this day and age. So what if the practical science we know and work with is at a delay in catching up with the incorporation of mental evolution into human genetics?

But, mental evolution how? Haven't we been told that our human predecessor was a bit clumsy, somewhat apelike? How is it they were knowledgeable enough to design and conduct such a feat?

Coming into the picture of the physical and mental development of the race, we must simply acknowledge that, a human similar to the one encountered on the streets today couldn't have possibly completed the prehistoric structures with their bare hands. Yet we understand that they didn't have access to the modern machines that we have today product of our scientific and mechanical advances.

It is a fact of science that a race of giant could not have devolved into a race of smaller people without a genetic mutation of the entire race. At least it seems very unlikely that a mutation of the entire race of giants could have taken place. Also very intriguing is the coincidence of the development of sophisticated equipment concomitantly with the reduction in physical size and strength in men.

It is evident that the reduction in physical size resulted in enlargement of the mental capacity allowing for the substitution of muscular force by that of mechanical achievement. Napoleon was a very little guy with an enhanced mental capacity whom achieved a feat that he THOUGHT of being the need of his time.

Since thought precedes action, and it does. If action has an impact on memory, and it does. A prior generation recording in its memory banks the future requirements of humanity regarding the suitability and adaptability of oncoming generations is by conciliation of thought. Simply put, projecting into memory is enhanced by mediation of thought.

The human soul, which we accept as a reality, is none less than a gigantic memory bank that stores the actions and thoughts of the human unit. When a collective of souls has stored similar actions and needs, then there comes the change or mutation or enhancement of DNA needed to effect a physical and mental suitability.

It all evolves from the creation of the physical component of the human. Taking from the physical strength that people in the past needed to have, in order to cope with the needs of the day, then we presume that their cranial composition wasn't as relevant as their physique.

Very many were endowed with physical strength and aptitude and not so many had the enhanced mental capabilities that an individual as Napoleon did exhibit. Obedience and devotion to hierarchy had to be the necessary sentiment of the masses in the day of the giants of which Goliath descended from. In the highest level of consciousness was the duty to please a higher order.

When an accident didn't alter the course of life, exhaustion from hard work had to be the necessary cause of death. Giants must have had a hard life for a very long time before they were able to record in their gigantic soul memory that size and strength was their demise.

But the human race had been concocted into existence to stay! And if the development of a refined cerebral activity was necessary, the human was designed to evolve into it.

Slowly but surely. Time we have as much as we need. There is no end to time. A term may be reached and a new one begins.

Plan ahead carefully and mistakes are still liable to occur, but there is one sure way to stay steadily on course without doubts. Mental awareness of time and action. It deters previous mistakes from reoccurring.

Reaching quiet of thought assures an accurate and steady evolution. But since the entire race isn't going to achieve quiet of thought, in one generation, those few that do have to suffice for the rest of us. They have a sacred duty to spread the knowledge and make disciples of all.

The best way to make fishers of men is by instilling awareness into their consciousness. That is when a portion of the subconscious becomes conscious. That is when an aware collective's consciousness is stored into the soul, altering the DNA of the dormant brute into the conscious refined human. That is when the following generation is born DNA ready for acceptable change.

The Roman Empire came to be as a result of obedience and devotion to hierarchy being the sentiment of the masses. Was it necessarily an unavoidable step of submissiveness in the evolution of human consciousness?

To develop the hunger for independence and sovereignty of the self, must many first be subject to the domination exerted upon the collective? Is such the reason explaining why humanity has surrendered for so long the domination of wealth at the hands of the powers that be?

The three strongest military superpowers on the planet, in 2019: in first place The Americans with their Allies, in second place The Russian, and in third place come The Chinese. The United States is the wealthiest country by far, secondly comes China and many slots behind is Russia.

Analyzing the three colossuses, The United States of America is the youngest nation of the three and it does not have the most territory nor does it have the most inhabitants. Its military and its economy surpasses that of every other nation because it was born out of oppression to be a Republic and it has maintained its Republican mission. It was born to allow acceptable freedom in all of its expressions. As evil it may be seen as, it has a history of treating its people with the most fairness and respect, qualities not always found in other free nations.

The United States of America has historically been a faithful ally to many countries and dignitaries; at times a formidable adversary, to be dealt with, for several others as well. Its founding fathers set out for the distinction of its people and the land. Through the years its forces have protected the people of many nations from their own tyrants and have averted threats invading from other borders.

The US has created extraordinarily good and strong institutions for the welfare of its own. For many decades it has been the leader of the free world. But the real reason for its military and financial success is due to the people that have fallen in love with the country and its institutions.

The United States has the love and trust of its people behind it. The USA is yet a very young nation, under three centuries old. The Roman Empire lasted fourteen centuries from its first emperor to its last, and the first two centuries were totally peaceful.

The Emperor and his loyal advisors had the power of domination over the population. His generals and the army commanders were all roman citizens. It was a title of nobility to be called a Roman Citizen. Yet, after that many centuries of spread domination the empire lost support and collapsed. A seed of conscious rejection to the domination had opened its petals into a large portion of the collective.

The base of its support was maintained by excessively taxing the people. The people paid to stay under domination. Same domination most governments impose today with the added ingredient of ignorance and illiteracy in a time of light and luminaries.

Capitalism is taxing people to exhaustion and communism starves them to the grave. Capitalism should have been envisioned as flourishment of a system of currencies and not as a per capita punishment. Blood draining tax collection is evident in the early decades of the twenty first century.

The Roman Empire lost support and weakened. It was taken over by the so called barbaric legions; sick to boredom from tax paying and contribution of their labor in the roman public works.

In all fairness it must be admitted that the romans also contributed in the organization and modernization of prosperous nations of today.

World powers such as England and France, Spain and Germany and many other nations of relevance in the world arena of today sprung out of Roman domination; nonetheless, The Empire lost support and perished.

The United States must be on the lookout that the barbaric legions don't weaken its institutions. Do not allow overburdening of its capabilities to the point of confusing its aim and dethroning the land of milk and honey. Those with their trust in love and respect for freedom and prosperity around the globe shall give true meaning to such statement. The Republic must stay prosperous and strong and sensible in order to continue being the leader that it needs to be.

Let the true leaders of the Nations consider the contents herein and apply as many a remedy as necessary. Partisan quarrels stemming from personal agendas are to be put aside for the best interests of the nations.

It is time that greater nations stop the handouts to smaller nations and lead the way instead. Handouts create a state of dependency making it harder for poorer countries to harness their responsibility to the people, and it serves as an incentive to acts of corruption.

Handouts do not allow for the people to grow love for their soil and as a natural result pour away from their borders. Do not blame the grizzly in search for honey when it invades your territory if you placed the honeycomb outside your door.

If an emergency arises, if the greater is slaughtering its own, by all means please help. Standing by is inhumane and the people shall be grateful for the assistance. Beyond that, allow each people in its own culture to learn how to love and care for each other and prosper as a result of their own institutional progress.

CHAPTER TWO

THE CONSCIOUS HUMAN

The human race is undoubtedly one of the last breathing beings to have been inserted among the great number of species that conform the world's population. Scientists estimate the number of species at about 8.7 million, and continue to speculate that about 80% of species have not yet been discovered. Where could they be concealing themselves?

Of all the earthly creations mankind may very well be the most dependent of nature. If the human species isn't a usurper of power, there exists a very high probability that Creation intended for Homo sapiens to be in charge. To be in charge and to share the land with other forms of life: plant, animal, fungi, etcetera. Being in charge brings the responsibility of carefully exercising its expanded analytical abilities for universal benefit.

A superior being with the ability to evolve into conscious knowing of itself and its surrounding. The Homo sapiens was probably just a simple experiment up to the point where self-awareness earned us free will. A creature such as the human had to be worked upon until minimum intellectual qualities where achieved, and from that point on liberated to its own volition.

While initially truncated many times, the human experiment must have consisted of some sort of an ambitious and unique lab project of a higher consciousness. A responsible lab project intended to express a highly evolvable species with aims of acquiring qualities comparable with an unselfish maker. A Creator that aspired the fabrication of a creature capable of evolving to maker-status.

A common dictionary definition of an animal reads as follows: a living organism that feeds on organic matter, typically having specialized sense organs and nervous system and able to respond rapidly to stimuli.

Probably, many a times, the initial human species attempts were just that. A common dictionary definition replica of an animal. When it started recognizing itself being different than the rest of the kingdom, that's when it began opening up to the superiority of itself as a species. It then started feeling love and compassion for the rest of nature. Respect and fear just as much.

In addition, the human animal must also possess a thread of uniqueness. A thread that bonds the physical aspect of the self with the more subtle mental and sensorial capacities, which runs out of one human being and into the next. In such a way connecting the entire human race with its local environment.

Through association the local environment connects with the rest of the planet and beyond. Taking from their exhibited state of evolution, some human beings are assuredly better integrated within themselves and seemingly more connected to their habitat than others.

The functional organic basic unit that makes up the physical components of the body, the cell, must have conscious molecules conforming it. The autonomous functions of the body must comprehend certain level of conscious communication among the brain and the performing organs.

Pretend that you're wanting a verbal interaction with someone you just met that does not have auditory capability or that simply doesn't understand your language; all of which you're unaware of. The communication process will not be very fluent between the two because the latter will not be able to respond in kind. Differently, the autonomous functions of the body continue to happen as if it were the brain in the skull communicating to a brain in each cell of the organs.

Let's say you become conscious of your breathing process and decide to stop breathing, just for a few seconds. Then you consciously continue to inhale and exhale for a short period, totally awake to the exercise. You are then controlling the routine of breathing for as long as your lung capacity allows you to. After a while you disconnect your consciousness from the activity and forget about it. The communication of the cells in the lungs with the brain and the circulatory system continue to happen and the demand and supply of oxygen takes place without you manipulating it. Those cells that conform the chest organs are conscious of a cellular intercommunication with the neurons and perform their response. Every animal in the kingdom does that, but not every animal can make the conscious analysis we make here. So far, as much as we know, only the human is capable of such consciousness.

There is people that care deeply and have made big sacrifices for the betterment of humanity. We owe to Nicholas Tesla, for example, many of the advances we've currently achieved. They are a consequence of his dedication to demonstrating the benefits of alternate current despite mainstream belief favoring direct current. He was ridiculed at the time of his exposition and died in poverty, but anyhow his theories have proven to be accurate.

Mr. Tesla believed that future society deserved to live in a changed and more comfortable environment. His connection with the whole of life made him more conscious and aware of the benefits that science and nature have in store. Thus he was able to tap into certain knowledge that was totally obscure and hidden to his contemporaries.

It is an autonomous mission of the race to become ever more conscious of the connectedness to ourselves. To our integration as a people, as a planet and as a universe. Only by staying consciously linked can we give the free will responses that each era requires of us and thus evolve as a race.

A human being cannot be detached from its relatedness. It is an impossible and it is totally unviable. It is understood as a natural occurrence that we each are physically separate persons, bodily independent from each other, with the freedom to associate with one or another.

Nonetheless and adjacent to each of us, exists a common space that blends into our corporal limits and exerts a gravitational push that keeps us all standing on the same ground. It continues to happen even when consciousness differentiates us into more or less evolved individuals. Individuals that through consciousness create a force to contrast against the push that presses a ceiling over our growth.

Beyond the conscious line of self lies an unconscious extension of ourselves into one another and unto all else. That barrier between consciousness and unconsciousness is the one we are called to lower to imperceptible levels.

In that same sequence of thought we can express that our planet earth undergoes the same relative circumstance of connectivity. Having its physical boundaries: above, below, and periphery experimenting the same blending of its outer limits with the surrounding space and the atmosphere that houses every celestial body. As a result our earth and every other heavenly solid are all extensions of each other.

Our planet is a large chunk of land that houses immense oceanic pools that seem to isolate the land into separate units. The larger continuous expansions of land we call continents: Africa, Antarctica, Asia, Australia, Europe, North America and South America. The smaller portions we call islands.

It is no secret that the land only appears to be separated on the surface of the waters because the bottom of the oceans is a continuation of the continents and islands. Imagine the craters on the moon at some point holding massive bodies of water separating large portions of land.

Now picture that thread of uniqueness we mentioned earlier which runs through one person and into the next, and compare it to the large chunk of land that our planet is. Well... similarly to the waters which can't prevent the land from staying connected underneath of its surface, we people being unique and distinct personalities can't separate from each other and from all that is because of that unbreakable bond that threads us together to all that is.

It so happens because that thread, that same thread that unites all people, grounds us all to the land and connects the land to the waters and the waters to space. It maintains each celestial body in its orbit and envelopes all things in the roundness of its unending confines. It even contains the heavy oceans from spilling its waters when the earth in its normal orbit presents the oceans facedown into empty space. Amazing! A very strong thread. Isn't it? It is not only the moon that affects the mood of the tides, don't forget that the earth in its rotation, translation and roundness would easily shed all of its contents were not for the thread that keeps gravity in check.

Creation intended for each one of us to be intertwined with the rest of our kind, with all that is and with It. Keep in mind that it is our right and duty to evolve individually and as a conglomerate of people and things. Also remember that those persons that attain higher levels of consciousness in and of themselves and of their affinity and interdependence with each other, if they so choose, may assist the global community in its efforts of awakening to higher levels of conscious unity with all that is.

Certain human qualities are transmitted to us from our parents and from their ancestors at the time of birth/creation and other qualities we must evolve into. Very much the same as material life is given/approved unto us it is our right and duty to make the best of our individual selves and the best in the global community with the rest of all of life.

We are meant to grow our community and to grow in our communities. We're not born holding hands, yet we learn to hold hands and lend a hand because it's all part of our evolutional selves. Evolution is engrained into our DNA and we continually evolve.

Whether we do so by design or not, it is entirely up to us, as individuals and as a social conglomerate.

Allow at this point for a few clarifying words. That which is intended for you, the reader, to understand when it is mentioned that we humans probably having been solely an experiment up to the point when we had gained self-awareness. Also, when it is professed that being a detached human being is an impossible and totally unviable. And lastly, when it is pronounced that just the same as material life is given/approved unto us.

In retrospective order: when saying that material life is given/approved unto us, we should realize that we must then already exist. We must already exist in some shape or form in order to be eligible to take on or be granted permission to receive or accept something. Our physical bodies in this particular case.

Granting the knowledge of our physical bodies being manufactured in the world we see and touch and through a process that most adult parents understand, then our prior form of existence must be from a less dense reality.

Let's get practical stating an example in a situation we can all attest to. Brain surgery for example. The scientist can always reach in and grab a chunk of the brain, but they haven't figured out how to pull thoughts out of the brain. Yet we know that there are thoughts going through our heads. So thoughts must exist before the physical brain does, and after the brain is, because the matter of the brain perishes and the thoughts continue to be long after.

That place where thoughts are created and generated out of is what in this book is referred to as Creation. Exactly, you guessed correctly. The exact same place that we hail from before we inhabit our physical bodies.

That combination of brain and thoughts is what makes up the human mind and that combination of a somewhat dense human physical body and Creation is what conforms, makes up, the Human Being. Just to give you a glimpse of how great you are, by being able to procreate a physical human body you have been given Creator abilities. You yourself are a co-Creator.

In saying that being a detached Human Being is an impossible and totally unviable means that when taking into consideration that we already exist as some kind of Being before being granted a physical body, then in becoming a Human Being...or human system... we are then a combination of more than one component and separation of the one from the other would render us back into the original unit and no longer a human person. This all takes us back to being interconnected and dependents of each other. There is no human possible way to thrive as a society if we don't all lookout for each other. It's just how it was meant to be.

Lastly, when uttering that we humans probably were just an experiment up to the point where we gained self-awareness, refers to the superiority of physical matter. That superior DNA nomenclature necessary to allow the blending in with that Being we emanated from. That Vital Force we emanated from and are a part of. That Existence that is the core of who we were before and will continue to be after our physical density setting foot here on the planet.

Knowing that, we're lifelike. That the core self that we are infuses life into the dead of matter. Although it isn't really dead, only in-animated. Then and only then do we evolve from the unconscious blend of being and matter into the conscious unity of ourselves and with all that is.

Only in possession of this awareness do we become godlike co-Creators and evolve into ever more and higher states of consciousness.

In the process of elevating ourselves we lift up with us those that have not generated of their own doing the state of awareness that we have achieved. Creating and endless chain reaction of those on top ever climbing to higher states of consciousness and unity with all that is and exists, while making room for those below to occupy the seats we vacate out of.

These stages of evolution are absorbed by the physical components of the whole as well as by the-none-physical components such as the substance that thoughts are made of.

Coming upon this knowledge of consciousness of ourselves and the fellow human, creates the inevitable responsibility of providing for those in the lower stages of evolution. A responsibility of unity that we have eluded for too long a time, of unity and awareness with the surroundings and with all that is.

Everything that we can do, we must do. We must strive to keep the Intellectual Collective free from Ignorance, Disease, Homelessness and Hunger. It must be achieved without further hesitation

CHAPTER THREE

FOUR COMMON HUMAN NEEDS

Eating, sleeping in a protected shelter, processing health and becoming wiser are things we need to do even if we don't intend to. Although, not in a uniform fashion all these are automatic human requirements. Society must ensure the natural process of keeping the human vehicle and mind at its best. Not making provision for such a need at a social level, this day and age, is inhumane to say the least.

When Homo sapiens first appeared on the face of the earth, each adult person would procure their own livelihood and that of their dependents. In today's social structure the Intellectual Collective has empowered the institutional empire and thus lost its personal management of the resources at hand.

The fear of losing its possession allowed the individual to entrust control of the fruit of their labor to the Establishment. The Establishment, first in an innocent approach and later becoming very aware, manipulated the degree of ignorance and of knowledge available to the Collective.

The Establishment is one of the best administrative tools that society has come upon. Nothing wrong with the Establishment as a means. But, from being a useful tool to the system it has grown into a powerful machine that overrides the needs and wants of its creators. All which renders it dysfunctional and will cause an inevitable collapse of the structures in place.

When a tree grows overly leafy it must be pruned so that its roots could continue to support the weight of its branches. If the branches of the tree grow too fat and long, eventually sunlight, oxygen and necessary nutrients cannot reach the roots and the cortex rots and dries up causing the tree to drop altogether.

Have we reached a great height of civilization? According to recorded history we're the most advanced civilization that has ever existed. Have we gone far enough? Should we stop evolving now? No and no. We have upon our shoulders the responsibility of resolving the world's most pressing human issues.

When we do it and how we accomplish it? It is our choice. But, how much we do? Is not. The same concept of no end of times applies to the evolution process. There's no ending to how evolved we may become. We are godlike and God is endless and unlimited in all aspects. If there were an ending to our evolution, the entire human race would have already been vanished from the face of the earth.

Let's not be complacent because a minority of people has accomplished many goals. Accessibility for all to a world of opportunities and achievements is what will give peace and everlasting pride to the few forerunners heading the relay. Once they are physically retired some of us have to grab the baton and continue on with the race.

Maybe not having a conscious knowing of the perpetuity of material life on the planet is what has triggered in the past the notion of a world ending by fiat of Deity. Last thought to happen by 2012, and by year 2000 before that.

Just to be somewhat illustrative allow me a personal anecdote here. My great grandmother lived to be 103 years of age. She being the oldest person in my family and still productive, everybody went to her for advice. I recall that while I was still a young boy, around ten or eleven, I went up and asked if it was true that the world was going to end?

Take into consideration that great grandma was a very knowledgeable lady. I was too young to evaluate her talents, but she was known for curing many of the ailments that affected the rural community. She knew many of the plants that healed broken bones and that brought health back to the sickly. Also she was the midwife for all the parturient women of her region.

The topic of the end of the world was a big concern to me, even as a young boy, because it's something that I kept listening to over and over again. Back in the day rumors spread mostly through radio broadcast and by word of mouth. Now a days children have the internet, but in my childhood, children consulted with their elders. Well, she confirmed my fears, yes she replied. That it was nearing the end. She said it would end in 1983. You can't imagine how terrified I was.

I was very terrified. So much so because, and according to her account, it had once ended with a deluge and a few had managed to survive. She didn't want to scare me, but she was certain it would end. So that time it would be swept by fire and everyone would be gone. Guess what! Coincidentally, she passed that year, in 1983. But did the world end? Mine came to a halt for a little bit, but the world kept on turning.

The Intellectual Collective out of ignorance of their own fate has worked and contributed to the good living of a now large minority. Out of ignorance because it's only obvious that if everyone had been intellectually equipped, all at once to the same abilities, then no one would have volunteered to anyone else's advancement. Sounds selfish and it shouldn't be, but it's true.

Imagine that race of giants we mentioned earlier. Had they been as sagacious as the rest of the order, they would not have volunteered to the physical struggles they underwent for the distinguishing of their society. Highly skilled laborers now a days have life insurance, workman's compensations, great salaries and excellent retirement plans.

It is safe to say that Creation in seeking the natural evolution of the race allowed for a few to be better driven and motivated for success. How else would we become godlike if not by being and letting be.

So now that consciousness is ripe, we all acknowledge how greatly the vast majority of the population has contributed to the enhancement of a greater minority worldwide since ancient history. Being godlike, it's only reciprocal for the powerful few to pull the Intellectual Collective out of its misery. Out of its misery and into glorious rejoice of a great and exhaustive Nutrition, Shelter, Health Care and Education systems.

This book is taking the people and the gubernatorial institutions of every country on the face of this earth, most importantly, through the very simple process of achieving it.

An education system provided by the community to its members. A system where the educators come from out of the womb of the community. One in which the educator's children can fearlessly attend the schools in the communities their parents teach in.

A health care system in which third world countries and their health authorities and providers care about the restoration to health of the individual patient. A system where life threatening emergencies are treated without questioning. An arrangement where monetary payments are never an issue, but a guarantee. A process in which each patient is ensured through facial recognition and total health restoration is the only permissible concern at the time of admission of an emergency situation.

A robust construction mechanism capable of erecting shelter on demand so not a single citizen goes homeless and susceptible to the inclemency of weather and criminal activity. Temporary go-to homes where individuals and families can take cover during emergency or distressful circumstances.

Adequate nutrition in every stage of life is relevant to proper physical and mental development. Starting with gestation the mother and the child should stay well-nourished for adequate completion of the pregnancy and consequent delivery.

During infancy, childhood and adolescence, a close monitoring and revision of the individual's food intake is to be an adhered to agenda. Children need vitamins and proteins for physical growth, bone strength and proper development. Good sleep enhances expansion of mental capacity and the learning abilities. During these stages the tutoring of the appropriate habits, acceptable social behavior and domestic compliance is necessary.

The adult person should stay nourished according to the levels of energy consumption due to work and physical engagement. Old age has its food intake requirements and should be met according to standards.

Compliance with the basic needs of the individual in the categories of Nutrition, Shelter, Health and Education is preliminary to the individual's wellbeing. It is preventative of unwanted circumstances in every scenario of the physical and mental stability and the psychological realms. It is beneficial to all that every member of every social circle have their basic needs satisfied.

Deprivation of proper nutrition promotes social outbreaks that materialize in the form of mischief such as theft and physical assaults. This is serious matter. Many innocent citizens have resulted with injuries and several more have lost their lives due to acts of vandalism. The loss of lives and physical disabilities resulting from such social behavior causes orphans and the cycle recycles.

CHAPTER FOUR

A SYSTEM OF WRONGS

In today's social economics what happens is that the authorities react instead of taking a proactive approach on the adverse happenings. People are taken into custody and processed into a system of lesser values. The dead are vengefully mourned and the injured worsen due to a lack of an affordable healthcare system. It is a clear picture that education has not been a priority in the system of wrongs.

Such a system of wrongs is self-destructive and self-degenerative. Society as a whole reverts to a more primitive form over time. Everybody finds someone to blame when the only culprit is a degenerating system of wrongs upheld for the wrong concepts. Concepts that will end up annihilating its upholders.

Many may even argue that the diverse social economic platforms and the variances adopted by each of its host nations is suitable to their ideologies. Must we be reminded that such ideologies created by a few well intended humans are only an experiment up until it's a free will choice of all the participants involved? It can't be a free will choice of all until the same basic threshold is afforded to all.

Not one individual or establishment should be allowed to own the high end portion of the system and not one person or social group should be handed the low end portion of the system.

100% of the world's population has the right to an equal threshold. All markers should be set at CERO: Cero hungry people, cero homeless, cero poor health and cero ignorance.

Only with such basic indicators of wellbeing and prosperity will our civilization be able to come in touch with and participate in kind with the likes of encounters that the explorer of space expect to find.

It is of an intellectual assumption to accept the fact that among other interests the nations are competing in their exploration of space in the hope to encounter intelligent life outside of this world. This world we inhabit and which we call home.

What are we going to share as a planet? Hunger, homelessness, disease, ignorance? What kind of respect shall we command? Are we going to smuggle our destitute among the different spatial spheres? Are we going to be found so lowly civilized as to be dealt with as the conquerors did the aborigines of the Americas?

If strength does not reside in the people then our civilization is weak. But this is a weak civilization because our nations are powerless. If Russia, China and The United States is what we have for show then we're doomed. All three are infected by indigence. After the People read these facts and their Institutions practice the precepts herein, it is many that shall be eager to learn which nation will be the first to raise the flag of all markers set to cero

Furthermore, the compliance with all markers set to cero is very much in favor of a powerful group that is already squandering great resources to combat crime, mental illnesses, and all kinds of illegalities. Delinquencies that range from petty crimes perpetrated by the regular citizen to high levels of corruption exhibited by many incumbents in the official sectors. Assets are mainly being misspent in providing temporary relief to an evil that is not going to go away unless it is correctly and definitively wiped out.

Most countries and their politicians only recall their responsibility to the core of the population during the times of electoral concern. Immense amounts of capitals are misused supporting endless numbers of political parties and organizations. Too much money is burnt up a chimney stack in campaigning and in pursuit of the voter's favor; sufficient wealth that could find use in empowerment of the pauper to generating the means leading to satisfying their own basic requirements.

It is not unheard of that politicians throughout well-known parts of the civilized world finance their electoral campaigns with money from illicit activities. Later during their mandate said elected officials incur in the laundering of their benefactor's assets. Many get off with a slap on the wrist and in some situations the population is utterly kept in the dark.

How abusive a manipulation of the people's sacred needs forcing the Intellectual Collective into mind numbing habits. Perpetuating crime and delinquencies within their own borders because power must be had and retained at the people's expense. Such leaders must be questioned as to how whole they are in their makeup and integrity. How are such leaders complying with their quota of elevating humanity in as much as their investiture requires of them.

The Intellectual Collective should be fed truthful information about each candidate. The polling process should be scanned by an electoral college. An electoral college in which each member has initially been voted in by the population in their communities of origin. A community of origin in which they have already served a required length of time before they are allowed to serve in a national capacity.

An Electoral College member must be known to all and should act in representation of the members of their community of origin. An Electoral College member must be one that remains subordinate to a congress of community members. Exactly the same community congress that said public servant originally emanated from when joining the Electoral College.

An electoral college put together in such fashion has the best interest of the community at heart and is one that has the best interest of the nation at heart. Experience has proven that the vice versa concept does not always render true.

Serving each community for a greater nation is what the Intellectual Collective deserves from its elected officials. A centrally located congress in a nation's capital does very little for each and every community. A centrally located congress in a nation's capital is detached from the community it has pledged to represent and serve.

Let the Presidents and their Cabinets serve from a remote location. The executive is the one and only head of state and it would be impossible to make themselves present the entire time in each community. It makes no difference where they sit or stand because at home or abroad they are the executive authority.

The Presidency should always be aided while equally monitored by the Electoral College in order to provide balance in government.

The Electoral College must be an organism that is present to approve or disapprove of the actions to be taken by the executive. Providing that the Electoral College is at all times in coordination with the congress of the community back home, all actions decided upon in government will have approval or not in the community.

The congressional team will in turn be in direct contact with the community through its leaders. Community leaders should be the lowest bracket in government to be elected casting a vote.

Many community volunteers ranging from the ranks of students, teachers and academic professionals to the business engaged adults will serve as liaison between the community and its leaders. The community leaders will be subject to the volunteers in its communication with the congress of community members. Decision options run up to government and execution runs down from government.

Communication and delegation are very effective tools aiding the Presidency. As far as the highest elected official whom is also the Commander in

Chief of the Armed Forces is in constant communication with their cabinet, with their generals and the Electoral College, they're liable to do a decent job. The rest is a matter of good decision interpretations and great international business relations. This alone keeps the head attached to the body members it presides over.

The Executive in charge of Office is 100% more involved in governing than the minute description we allow in these pages, but the establishment needs not be as large and costly. It absolutely doesn't have to be half as complicated as it seems to be today. One factual data indeed is that these chapters are intended to be acknowledged by every- and-all nations that incubate starved, homeless, diseased or ignorant indigents within their borders. Exempt are all those with all markers set at cero; throw the first stone those without sin.

The Electoral College performs the job of supervising the polling process and once the president takes over the presidency they work alongside the executive making sure their congress back home is kept abreast of the decisions of government. In this manner the communities, through the work of their electoral appointee, can remotely participate; communities corroborate, or disapprove of government decisions affecting the Intellectual Collective.

In the sectors of government as we know it today, institutions such as congress and the electoral colleges must redefine their functionality. Governments must be reduced in size while becoming cost effective.

The population through their appointee in the Electoral College has to have direct participation with the presidency in the endeavors of civil matters. Many benefits are achievable through a congress in the community instead of in the nation's capital and an electoral college serving as liaison of the presidency all the way down to the center of the communities.

In today's political arena, Congress with all its might has forgotten its subordination to the people. Congress in today's society is acting more as a barrier between the Presidency and the people. It is mandatory, once and for all, that the legislators come closer to the communities. That they identify with the immediate needs of their commonwealth and feel the voting power of the Intellectual Collective that put them in office.

A prominent scientist has put together a robot that has grown a mind of its own. How is it possible that the Intellectual Collective has conceived an establishment to safeguard its very needs and now the installation has made hostage of its creator. Hostage for ransom. Fostering the intention of negotiating with the highest bidder. Usually ignorance being the highest bidder that runs away with the collective.

A congressperson goes to their post or not and the owner of the building is totally ignorant of the fact. Let's get back to working arms in arms with the people. Let's see our people in congress walk the streets without fear of contamination with the population.

The Intellectual Collective elects you to a well remunerated and prestigious job and in turn it is required of you to have the decency to stay connected with the people. You are no longer allowed to use paid time for your own leisure. The

Intellectual Collective has become aware of their rights and of your duties to them.

In the same manner that a human person cannot detach from its component parts without becoming inanimate matter, in that same manner an establishment has to stay connected to the source it emanates out of. Not proceeding accordingly has caused social unrest and disruption.

The Establishment as it is today, the world over, is totally responsible for the ills of society. Therefore it is only just that it rolls up its sleeves and gets to work. Get to work implementing an organic solution to the problem that it conveniently keeps in place while it still has the power to do so.

Putting a society together again after it has erupted has proven to be, in the conventional terms, a life consuming task. Past decapitation of the king has demonstrated that the people will get the attention it deserves. Giving back to its rightful owner that which is alien, is the only way to evolve peacefully and honorably.

The source, the core substance, the animation of government is the people. The source will always prevail. The Creation of life has decided upon it. It's just a matter of time and consciousness for an establishment that lacks the support and participation of the people to become inanimate, extinguished, vanished, gone.

Thus far, every so called democratic country has been playing the game of alternation of power. Stating that when their party is next in government they will correct the damages of the last. At least in the Americas, for the last two hundred years, it has all been broken promises and a bunch of lies.

The people don't need your promises. The people own you. Have you forgotten dear establishment? Clearly you have, but it's about time that you wake up to good memory. The people is now taking over and you will do the job you lobbied for, and were elected to do. Do you not remember that you swore before the bible and the people, so help you ....

A bunch of trained corrupts enticing half a country to support them. Support us now that when we reach power we will return the favor. All of the tax payers elect a government and not only the few that have direct communion with the Office.

Not even in the miraculous United States of America have the politicians learned that enough is enough. Stop lying to the people. Stop hiding behind the mistakes of the party in power. It has only been a subterfuge to reach power and then more of the same.

The loudest pitch is now telling you that the Intellectual Collective has caught on to the game and is no longer tolerant of the party bull! Cut the crap now, before it is too late.

It is very easy to debate in front of TV cameras when you haven't had the opportunity to run your own household yet. Much worse when they've been in office and lied to the public up and down and still get elected.

That serves as proof of how much damage can be done when the public is played with and is kept in the dark. Some of these countries are handing out a bottle of beer and a stick of salami on election-day. All in exchange for their voting documents. Especially when they are known to be of a different party than the one in power. That goes to show how hungry and deep in ignorance the population is being kept captive. Food for a day, numbing of the mind for a moment and ignorant and homeless for a lifetime.

Debating the current incumbents during electoral periods pointing out all the wrongs of their mandate is the thing of the day. They know the insincerity of their commitment to fix the wrongs. Most only want their run at the helm to best serve their appetite.

They speak a beautiful verb. Dishonorable politicians present themselves like the one that's going to save the nation. Only because their uncleanliness hasn't been highlighted yet. As soon as they convince the voters and assume power, immediately begin rubbing their hands. They are usually in complicity to the feast they are about to participate in. Governing a nation is a responsibility and not a privilege. Let the sovereign analyze, once your term is over, if it was a privilege or not to have you in office.

Nonetheless, the Intellectual Collective is coming to the understanding that a ruler can only be as effective and coordinated with the people's mandate as the established system allows. If everywhere one goes today everyone decries the establishment is because it needs to be recomposed.

The establishment this... the establishment that other thing. The president this...The president that. Some executives arrive at the establishment with great intentions. The same they announced throughout their campaign. Very soon after, the same people that voted them into power regretfully detest the President's actions and words. Their words may remain the same but their actions are not congruent with their campaign promises.

If for any reason, some particular president starts by fulfilling their campaign promises, then the opposing party in congress begins thwarting their actions. Seeking to have enough arguments to win favoritism for the next elections. The fight among the parties continues with only the Intellectual Collective owning the low end of the stick.

Congress needs not be a partisan body. Members of Congress should represent all the people in their communities. Not just their partisan affiliates' interests. Political parties must be allowed to assemble on their own without having interference in Congress or the Electoral College. Political parties already present their candidates to office. Parties should have more a schooling roll, in the view of preparing good candidates for the nation, and less a divisive one.

CHAPTER FIVE

INSTITUTIONAL EVOLUTION

The Establishment can only be as good as the institutions behind it. Having the required quantity of institutions is great. But, not every nation can afford the same number of them nor do they need the same amount of institutions.

Proper functioning of each institution is key. Do you see now the reason for some establishments being worse than others? Can you now peek at why the most powerful warmongers still have hungry, homeless, sickly and ignorant people on their streets? They have all the money in the world to go to war, plus an extra ten-years-worth of it: money that is. What's wrong with this picture?

INSTITUTIONS!!! They're in the wrong place, for the wrong reasons, and serving an erroneous purpose. A bunch of them: Banks and Clinics, Electoral Colleges and Congresses; Boards of Professionals and Political Parties, etc. We need to RECTIFY. Rectifying comes from experience and experience is expected from an evolving humanity.

After this long period of reflection, which started by the end of the French Revolution. A period in which the Intellectual Individual has allowed, accepted and complied with the status quo as it actually is. We are now ready to evolve into living a higher and more complicit state of affairs. A state of affairs in which the institutions we have created and endured with, find the humane functioning that our current consciousness invite into being.

The conscious ones among humanity have gained great awareness and capability of growth. With such acquired talents and abilities, how can any people among humanity conscious enough of this freedom of being, be lead into surrendering its innate ability to outdo and outgrow themselves? Sky is the limit says the popular axiom. It truly is when all free will beings are given unrestricted access to the undeniable right of fulfilling their basic living requirements.

It is known for a fact that Creation created a free will being with the ability to evolve genetically and mentally. Then, if the previous statement is factual, such a free will race of people had to be an otherwise physically limited species in relation to and in comparison with other earthly creatures. In the observation of nature there is not one creature that is ultimately and completely equipped.

A black, fiery eyed panther; for example, is capable of tearing up the human creature into a bazillion pieces. But guess what! The fragile human was out on a stormy day and saw the aftermath of when a streak of lightning struck the trunk of an old dehydrated tree bark. A fire broke out and the free will creature saw that the flame was impenetrable.

The Intellectual after much striking rocks against rocks was able to gather enough sparks and start a fire of his own. A fire that the black, fiery eyed panther could not penetrate and that shielded him from harm coming from the wild. Similarly, the Intellectual Collective after much struggle and endurance with the forces of its own creation, The Establishment, has come upon the definitive solution to its institutional breakdown.

Some limitations must the free-will, evolving and intellectual creature exhibit, in order to walk in the search of perfection. Perfection must then be the next step of complete. Perfection must then be a concept of relativity. Complete is what we were when Creation decided we could continue in the search for perfection on our own.

Perfection is a must achieve graduation in the gradual scale of consciousness, a higher grade each time. Perfection is only attainable by the creatively endowed, imperfectly complete, human state of being. A human that is totally unrivaled, even by the fiercest of creatures of the wild.

We humans, since our initial presence on planet earth, have demonstrated an eagerness to conquer. We go after the tallest mountain tops; we have descended into the scariest of abysses and even dared go swimming with hungry sea beasts. Athletes, scientists; artists, farmers; soldiers, scholars; all aspire to overcome and outperform our own standards.

Those with the wherewithal have plastic surgeries performed on themselves. Many exercise at the gym and practice yoga. Some eat healthy and do many things to better ourselves, our lives and that of our families and communities. Through our actions and conscious living we have the potential to enhance our nations and governments, our institutions and our place in material life. There is no question that everyone, at some point in their lives, has overcome obstacles that made them feel triumphant.

Most people have different interest and things that motivate them, but the one thing we all have in common is we all seek optimal nutrition, shelter, health and education for ourselves and for our next of kin. These basic needs must be satisfied to the fullest, perfection must be sought after and achieved in these endeavors.

Mother Teresa of Calcutta could not eradicate poverty from the face of the earth by herself, but she did a great job alleviating the sufferings of the many she encountered in a number of countries. Imagine all the greater good she could have accomplished, had her efforts been accompanied by the full support of each of those countries in which she contributed with her helping hands and got herself involved in.

So many big hearted people that have put their own skin into helping the cause against poverty. The battle went on and on and they never won. Want to know why? Because then and now they have been battling against a system that produces more and more of the same. A methodically organized production of a handful of affluent people and an unsurmountable ocean of necessitous people each time the Establishment changes a face.

There's a lot more wealthy people in the world today than there was last century, but the difference in comparison to the destitute is staggering. We must continue producing wealth while eradicating the lines of poverty. No one should stay hungry, homeless, ill, or ignorant.

What good is technology to the untaught? They can't save their lives if they have to execute a program on one of those expensive pieces of computer equipment in the windows of a retail store. What good is the large costly establishment to the homeless and uneducated? Is everyone in a secure place to sleep? Has the Presidency in any country ever declared a state of emergency to feed their hungry and cure the ailing?

Since many humans have not met the capability to fulfill their basic needs requirement, which in turn makes it difficult for them to achieve goals and thrive in life, it is imperative that the conscious and capable part of the population start rearranging the way our institutions function once and for all.

According to factual news report, supported by UNICEF In the last two months of 2018, two out of three children in the Central African Republic will not reach adolescence if they don't receive humanitarian aid.

The parents cannot farm the land because of the ongoing civil conflicts; civil conflicts arising mainly due to differing political and religious views. Disputes among agriculturalists and nomadic groups, as well as ethnicity also, being part of the disagreements.

A nation such as The United States of America has a population that comprises people from a vast array of political views and ethnic origin; the strength of its core institutions allows for a somewhat peaceful coexistence. Yet, not everyone in such a great nation has a guaranteed and uninterrupted access to food and shelter, healthcare and quality education.

So, what is we humans are doing so wrongly? How is it we're not evolving? What is keeping us stuck? Why aren't the most powerful nations completely successful at eradicating poverty all together among its population? What is keeping the human race from evolving in the matters pertaining to its basic living requirements?

Why are the so called poor countries in need of help from abroad? Let's take another look at The Central African Republic; for example, they have the ability to raise and export coffee, cotton and even diamonds are found among their natural resources. Are they really devoid of natural abundance? Well, the answer is obvious; they are only in lack of strong institutions willing to adopt the proper procedures.

Venezuela in South America has one of the most abundant oil reserves in the world. As of December 2018, South America's oil producing country is far from providing the minimum living standards to its more than 30 million inhabitants.

We are totally convinced that many countries are making a great effort to end hunger and homelessness, disease and ignorance, all together. Problem is they haven't gained access to the formula that will allow the rich and wealthy to stay rich and wealthy, while at the same time opening up the ports for the indigents to pull out of their rock bottom position and start climbing to an ever higher stadium of prosperity.

Taxing the wealthy to extend a handout to the needy isn't going to take us anywhere. The rich need to keep the engines running so that everybody can become productive. That's what this book is about.

As long as there exists a portion of the population that goes hungry and unsheltered, ill and ignorant, there is no chance on earth for anybody to become prosperous. It is only a matter of time before the rich and wealthy finish losing all they own to widespread disease, crime and corruption, war and violence.

Everyone will not be driven to entrepreneurism or to own property, but those that feel the rise of ambition in them will have the opportunity to achieve their goals. In diversity and in being able to choose resides the beauty of life.

Not everybody is called to pursue a college degree; many prefer to raise cattle or to grow food on a farm. They will all achieve their goals with the support from the institutions. The institutions that will invest and train, guaranteeing bonanza and making success a tangible reality.

The new institutional aspects of society will be more than drooling to participate because of the great impulse it's going to create in every sector of the economy. Therefore, an abundant source of wealth will be available for the demand and consumption of products and services.

Success is rolling on wheels! The world is being exposed to a primary formula that creates a solution to the prevailing basic needs situation. The approach promotes growth, respect and independence for the people, the institutions and the Establishment.

Governments grow stronger and more stable because of the pruning of its many leafy branches. The Intellectual Collective reaps the benefits of a no-handouts-accepted, all-integrated, all-concatenated, transparent system of government that allows the pride of providing for its own needs.

The Intellectual Collective Economic System promotes private property and the free enterprise; gets along perfectly well in any cultural setting and it doesn't interfere with tradition. It is a matter of human values, priority to the human and above all it is the matter of effectively initiating the next step in the necessary evolution of our current institutions.

Those great nations that provide most effectively for their Intellectual Collective boast great pride when they compare their achievements against the less organized countries. They should be proud. They have every right to boast because those countries are the ones with stronger social values, better priorities and stronger institutions. But they also continue to produce hungry and homeless people that are disease ridden and ignorant of what's best for them, the community and the entire nation.

The key factor resides in rehabilitating the institutions that we already have to fit the demands of the evolving Intellectual Collective. It is known that when the individual falters and falls under the wagon the norm calls for personal rehabilitation. According to the fault an institution is prescribed and the individual begins to be an intern for a period of time consonant with the fall.

It is also very noticeable that many people that falter once and recuperate due to their diligence to become institutionalized, a large percentage of the time; after a period of recovery, they happen to relapse. So what happens there?!? Simple! The system which is only as effective as its institutions is out of date. But why did the person falter the first time? Nine times out of ten, they fell through the cracks of an old and inefficient system.

It does not matter how strong the institutions may be. The bare fact that we, as a system, continue to produce indigents warrants fine-tuning the ways in which our organizations perform. Otherwise we are bound to continue failing. Failing in every effort we undertake in meeting the levels of satisfaction for achieving accessibility to the basic needs of all people around the globe. Failing is no more an available option.

Once we allow for the repositioning in functionality of just a few of our institutions, a small number in some countries and more in others. As it happens, the poorest of nations by the sole effort of its organizations shall be able to allot for the basic needs of its inhabitants.

This is a very positive step in our evolution because the competition of nation-against-nation, which we see in the global scenario today, will give way and come to a slow down if not to a complete stop. Then we will have a contest in which each nation will endeavor to become more and more efficient towards its nationals and less belligerent towards each other

CHAPTER SIX

THE IMMIGRANT

Can you imagine a world where the Intellectual Collective travels for pleasure and business and work, not as illegal immigrants? It is staggering the number of involuntarily displaced people in the world. People forced to leave their loved ones behind in search of a livelihood that would afford them the possibility to suffice for their young ones and for themselves.

It is hostile to say the least when human beings can't express their needs and wants because of a language barrier. Not being able to communicate properly makes them a victim of abuse and discrimination. Plus the fact that many times newcomers arrive at a city of which they know nothing about and everyone is a new face to them.

Being of a different culture, settlers find themselves being ejected out of their comfort zones. There isn't any blame of their own nor of the nationals from the countries and cities that they arrive into.

It is the nature of mankind to side with those of their same customs and ways of living. It gives people a sense of belonging, but that does not make them anti-anything or anyone. It's basically a topic that mainstream media has exploited because it sells commercials and they want to cash in on it. And of course it has taken afoot with a population that is vulnerable to manipulation. A certain period of assimilation is needed and afterwards the normal interaction among civilized people takes its due course. Most people with good social skills are rather warm and compassionate about the needs of foreigners.

Segregation most times than not is a natural process that occurs among any species as much as it does among humans. Homo sapiens join the bunch they feel most comfortable with. Such is a fact that those versed in the social sciences can attest to.

Very few mortals are educated in recognizing the ways and intentions of foreigners until those others take action and communicate. When immigrants don't speak the tongue, most times they stay amongst those they can interact with. It is a matter of fact that when their uncaring governments force them into exile, matters tend to worsen before taking a turn for the better.

Racist discrimination is not real or present among participants of different races that are raised together and in the environment of one same culture. They simply have nothing of fear towards tonalities of skin or facial features.

It is the fear of not knowing how somebody of a different culture, not a different race, will react to a particular stimuli that creates the aversion that promotes separation. A division that is initially voluntary until the fears of both towards each other dissipate. Such dread happens to evaporate in time and when the culture of the one is accepted or adopted by the other.

Whenever adult people of different cultures come together and are forced to coexist in a particular social setting, a safe distance and a dose of discomfort is kept during initial encounters. This occurs because of the rooting of each other in their respective cultures.

The informal exodus of a population towards other nations has created an enormous expense on the receiving nations. Most wealthy nations have inaugurated a social handout budget that is never enough for its own population let alone having to share it with the needful coming from abroad.

A social handout will never be enough because it was instituted as a means of pacifying a needy conglomerate and never as a solution. Believe it or not, it has served the purpose of dozing off the collective while the Establishment is ever larger and expensive.

The difficulty with a social handout is similar to the issue of consuming a fossil fuel. Gasoline is refined from finite resources and social handouts stem from finite institutions. Therefore, more tax payment is imposed over time and less are the goods and benefits to be received.

The Self is the one institution known to the Intellectual Collective originating in the infinite fount of Source. Only when the human is empowered to provide its own basic requirements will welfare cease to be a shameful social handout and the source shall remain inexhaustible. Remember that the Self is the basic Institution, mother of all other institutions, intrinsic to the Intellectual Collective.

Soon after the recognition, acceptance and empowerment of the Self-Institution takes place, in every nation, the immense quantity of resources being allocated today to persecute and process illegal immigration will terminate around the globe.

Shame on those countries that manufacture illegal immigrants and poverty as a byproduct of making a few citizens questionably rich. The vile, the corrupt ones. Shame on those countries! Sanctions should be imposed on them by the nations that have to provide asylum to the pauper of other lands.

Every country and their neighbor knows how costly it is to provide basic needs for a citizenry in today's institutional configuration. Nations around the world receive their nationals with deportation status without a moral flinch. If they were trying to own their responsibilities they should at least apologize to the nations that their people intrude into and sometimes commit barbaric actions.

It is a sensitive topic to be debated among the nations in question. A debate in the view of adopting the necessary preventative measures before border transgressions occur. Castigating the victims has been the most unfair norm. It has all been a very irresponsible treatment of an evil that is originally thrust upon those immigrants by their untouched governments. A chain is only as strong as its weakest link.

FORTIFYING THE WEAK LINK IS WHAT IS AT STAKE HERE

Human Rights organizations would be doing a very honorable job by paying attention to such happenings. Denouncing them before the proper court circuits would aid in coming up to a solution. When the resulting measures are not adhered to, then sanctions could be legalized for the unmoved nations. Hit them where it hurts the most. In the pockets of the deceitful. Initially their inflated bank accounts should be questioned and intervened if found to be fraudulent. All unearned income must be repossessed. The proceeds distributed among community banks in the localities where the returned immigrants can access. Those funds can be used to make them productive in their own towns of origin. Those countries which most citizens are fleeing from are statistically with very high levels of corruption in the ranks of their government officials.

It's such a shameful fact that it is the hungry, unprotected, ill and ignorant deportees that have to run up with the cost of leaving as well as the cost of returning to the same large and insensitive governments. Replete with shameless incumbents. Said countries should be penalized to the point where they would have to compensate their people for their hardships at home and abroad.

To every nation with a genuine desire to approach their institutional reorganization here is the formulation for doing it. This is the opportunity for the little ones to climb their status in Statehood. This is the opportunity for the current generation of politicians to make up for the pitiless change of times. This is the publication for the Intellectual Collective to understand and inform your elected officials. Inform your elected officials of the simple cost effective solution to institutional reassembly.

This means that less than developed third world countries will suffice for themselves. ABSOLUTELY! The formula in this book does not discriminate among nations or citizens. It encompasses every nation because all nations have institutions and they all possess wealth.

The grandest of all institutions is the Self. Honor yourself fully and allow the person that you are as many opportunities as you see fit. It's immaterial the number of times the individual has had to flee their country and returned against their will. The simple knowledge here will make your country a great and safe place to thrive in. Believe it or not, wealth comes with the Self. Many know this and many, many, many; are about to find out.

As a sample to the reader and in honoring myself writing this book, for example, comes from the Institution of my Self. Typing these chapters creates a fount of knowledge that is wealth by itself. Simply putting together these paragraphs expands the wealth of knowledge in the world. It promotes that people become more aware of themselves and of all the wealth that is emanating from them.

The nature of your birthing into humanity is for your own evolution into ever becoming a greater Self in every aspect of life. Including in the physical and material aspects which are the targets of these written words. Becoming wealthy and financially rich allows you to do much good in the world. Don't reject the opportunity.

Seek material wealth in as long as it doesn't harm you or others. If you incline towards spiritual values, which is the crib where the fount of wealth resides, look at it as a reward for being adept to good moral living standards and never oppose the course of your evolution.

Owning property and having material success was thought of in the moment Creation accepted the possibility of attaching a physical body to The Living You. And again arises the question. Do you imagine a world where the Intellectual Collective travels for pleasure, and business and work, and affords itself the luxury of not becoming illegal immigrants? And if perchance someone were to default in a foreign country, their nation of origin would be prosperous and willing enough to vouch for and fully repair their faults.

You can never imagine the immense quantity of resources being allocated in today's global drama just to persecute and process illegal immigration alone. Do you have any idea how much money Illegal immigrants all around the world pay just to arrive at their destination of choice? Billions and billions of dollars, money that can be spent to keep them at home. Monies that can be invested in growing their local communities.

The Gross Domestic Product of each nation should be estimated at the beginning of each fiscal year. Taken on a head count of its population and readjusted quarterly according to actual consumption and also on account of the remnants of the products and services in production.

At the end of the fiscal year the actual figures and the estimation shouldn't be too far apart. With the facts overlapping the projected production in an unfailing effort to provide for each and every individual in the economy.

Production should be kept at an adequate percentage above consumption in order to maintain fair pricing for local and national consumers. Once a nation provides enough for local consumption at accessible market pricing, only then should attempts be made to secure an international market for the excess in productivity.

Enough currency should be made available for each person through the banking system. The banking system is then the receptor and distributor of monies. The money engraving and printing bureau shall make the currency available to the banking system. Enough to avoid lack. Only small amounts of supervised paper currency is to be let out of national borders.

CHAPTER SEVEN

SPARK AND FUEL

This world and all of its beauty is organized to support human life; every inch of it is dedicated to bearing all the weight of humanity. Many millions of years have passed since the accounts of this earth being a sterile mass of gas and furious asteroids clashing and crashing against its surface and epochs of it being uninhabitable by the human races of today. Mortals only need to replenish the renewables that we deplete in order to keep the living planet green. If we don't contribute in returning to the earth the seed of its nature, then it will by itself find a balance. But, in the process of doing so, shortage may occur and it could be several generations before it becomes abundant again. In the interim a portion of the population may lack provision causing it to perish prematurely.

A potent sun shines in the beautiful sky up above. A starry night sky with grandiose and unending formations that a Benefactor or maybe a team of benefactors continue to design. Perhaps it is just such a vast canvas that we haven't finished uncovering it all. All of which we contemplate, admire in awe and believe affords being true.

Wonderful precipitations nourish and sustain the fruitful earth we walk upon; making it possible for rivers to flow providing free drinking water for all sorts of vegetation and animals including the human. The Intellectual Collective gets to play god and represses it. With the construction of dams creates reservoirs to administer its utilization converting its energy into electricity and other useful things because of its God-given ability to co-Create.

Vast oceans full of colorful life, flora and fauna, provide immense quantity of wealth and opportunities of exploration for the bold and audacious inhabitants of the land.

Every animal creature in the ocean, every bird in the air and every moving creature on land; every tree, every rock and every insect has its duties and responsibilities. Every unit of life has its freedom of being and provision for its every needs according to its relevance in the food chain.

The sky above is a thin ethereal film formation that allows movement in it. We are able to see the creatures and objects which altitude and speed is compatible with the reach of our sight. The fact is we only see the movement of the denser winged creatures that we call birds and some airplanes. Simply because they have the ability to navigate they stay up defying the down push of gravity. Gravity is just and only exerts a push equivalent to a balance in the mass of an object. Allowing for any effort greater than its mass to elevate it for as long as it can sustain its weight in the air.

The sky has its own decrees and principles; all it requires is obedience to its laws. Airplanes are built to comply with its principles and are permitted to navigate in it. Helicopters obey and are allowed to hover just like humming birds can.

It's difficult to say if the sky begins or ends at the farthest reach of human vision. In which direction is it really? The earth rotates on its own axis and around the sun, yet the sky is always looking up.

Sweet complicity between heaven and earth. The earth asks of it and the sky giveth. Plenty of rain fertilizing the roots of the land and providing nourishment to the shrubs and trees. The trees gratefully serve a nesting bed for the birds in the sky. Excellent symbiotic relationship between the sky above and the earth beneath.

How about the great and powerful oceans! Always arriving to kiss the shores of the land that it once covered in its entirety and yet very respectful of its boundaries as if a covenant to be and let be. A pact between two titans, water and land, blessed and sustained by the air above.

The air above provides its molecules for the waters to exist and the land to breathe. The air above that keeps the peace between the two colossuses, water and land, either by sharing itself in love or by expression of its might in gravity. A universal Law of Love and be loved.

Humanity didn't always evolve in a uniform way throughout and along each age. Certain civilizations have prevailed above others at one time or another. We have read that some have shown better technological advancements than others.

The Sumerians, The Phoenicians; The Egyptians, The Romans; The English, The French; The Spanish, all have had their contribution to the world along its history. Just to name a couple, the Sumerian left behind among other things the cuneiform writing system and the Phoenicians gave us an alphabet system which is the base for the alphabet we use today.

Many a nation has influenced another at one point in time or other. The Romans occupied modern day England, France and Spain. It was never a peaceful process, but after the waters returned to being calm, both people had gained knowledge from each other while sharing each other's culture.

The fourth Titan whom is a combination of creation and Creator is the human race. The human race that is so vulnerable and dependent of the other three, which are the air; the ocean and the earth, is yet a master above all three and of itself. A master above itself because of its innate ability to evolve each time into a greater and more conscious being.

The skies were created with a main purpose of breathing life into humanity, the earth to sustain it and the oceans to teach it respect for physical boundaries. The fourth titan as a creation is so very fragile to the violence of the rest of creation, but when it harnesses its creator-like abilities it can become a potent conqueror of all of it.

The human race was born totally fragile, still today we are able to attest to that, a prey at most. Frightened by a powerful animal kingdom. With no physical abilities to push back and frail to most climates and environments. The human race was confirmed with two of the most unique of conditions: fear and intellect.

Fear and intellect are two qualities that when used in combination with each other and harnessed as one tool, make up for one of the most awesome and powerful components available in the human arsenal.

In the initial stages of human sojourn on earth, fear was the spark that ignited the dormant intellect into action. Fear pushed humanity out of the wild and away from the reach of dangerous beasts. In such a move they came in the vicinity with less fearful animals that they were able to tame for their own benefit.

When fear is subdued by the intellect a bundle of great things is bound to happen. First let's make analysis of the intellect by comparing it with an engine. An engine capable of running on different fuels and let's look at fear as a necessary spark to start the engine running.

When the intellect is able to overcome the powerful and blinding spark of fear, it then dominates the course of action; the yield is going to be a conscious and a well measured result. A person acting in this manner is whom we denominate the intellectual.

Creation is a force which some may give the name of creative energy. A creative energy that is ever putting us in the middle of circumstances that will motivate us into a path of choices and growth. As we grow and evolve as individuals we want to make sure we are observing ourselves, our thoughts and our actions. We should always be in pursuit of conscious and well measured results in our lives and the lives of others.

Every thought that crosses our minds brings the intention to eventually give way to a productive image. Think of the brains as a womb that attracts and nurtures thoughts. In that same awareness thoughts mature and eventually exit the brain or step outside of our mentality and ardently seek to manifest into material expression.

Consequently such a complete thought will size up to sensitive tangibility. This means that we, or someone else in the present or in the future, will be able to see or hear; or taste or smell, or touch that thought of ours that has become a material thing or action.

Experience has already taught us that every action has a consequence. The benefit of a CONSCIOUS and a well measured result is that in such a fashion of acting we are able to trace back to the fuel that was the original spark to a particular result. This is how we control the outcome in the beautiful process of living.

We can make adjustments to our thought processes and our actions whenever we need to modify the result of a situation in life. So in this manner we are able to envision how wonderful and advantageous a dosed amount of fear can turn out to be in combination with the intellect. In fact, fear has been one of the greatest motivators of the intellect in effectuating many of the grandest improvements in human trajectory.

Countries with a strong climate change throughout the year have achieved great progress in home comfort. The people of such countries because of the fear of not having enough heat during the winter months have developed amazingly efficient mechanical heat production systems and equipment. When compared to many other nations located in regions with mild temperatures year round, they are very much more advanced and developed.

On the other hand, the intellect that is not simply triggered but it is totally overpowered by sudden fear, something that is unlikely to happen when living through the instances of life in a conscious and engaged manner, will allow a horrendous amount of wrongs to channel through and become materialized.

Regrettable abominations have occurred of which uncontrolled fear is to be the culprit of. When the actions resulting from this combination are prolonged for a period of time, then the engine which is the intellect could be running on bad fuel.

We have exposed fear as an initial spark that can trigger the intellect into a proactive course of action. That's the only kind of interaction we want to have with fear because that is as much as we can handle without entering into a reactive course of action.

When the intellect runs rich on fear, at which point fear isn't only a spark but also becomes the burning fuel of action that drives the intellect, then the intellectual becomes nervous, reactive and even dangerous. We don't want fear to stay dominant because it also has the property of becoming a bad fuel. The intellect running on inferior charge is the least productive thing that can happen to humanity.

Among one of the very unfortunate propellants that the intellect could be driven by is greed. Greed is universal, selfish and inconsiderate. It can sneak into the intellect without notice, a little bit at a time until it takes control of the entire decision making engine.

Getting rid of greed can be as tortuous as treating an addiction.

The fear of not acquiring enough of something has introduced greed into the human intellect. Being that greed is such a powerful and motivating fuel, and being that the human intellect has been endowed with the ability to overcome lack whenever satisfaction is its goal, then enough is sought and eventually achieved.

Once enough of whatever it is that the intellect has become greedy of has been obtained, then the fear of losing it kicks in. This creates an endless cycle of scarcity and then fear, greed and then having enough; which generates the fear of losing it again, and so on.

This endless loop of fear, greed; enough and then fear again, creates a state of chronic anxiety leading to the most commonly known disease of this age which happens to be stress. And a number of other illnesses of which medical science ignores the origin of and therefore very seldom is successful at finding a cure for.

Bad fuel is known to damage and dry out a good engine; the same goes for the intellect. But, what is happening with that massive portion of humanity that's lacking drive? Why are they lacking drive? Do they not fear enough? Too bold and stubborn maybe? Or are they not greedy enough?

CHAPTER EIGHT

ILL COMPONENTS

The lack of breakfast can ruin the day for somebody that didn't have a nutritious meal the previous night. The uncertainty of a protective home and no healthcare card in the wallet can render an individual to be unmotivated. Ignorance is a terrible tool to have when all else is lacking.

Numbing of the mind has become so popular that many are going to turn it into a currency of worldwide acceptance. It is so large the portion of the population that is lacking proper stimulation that they are willing to put their intellect to sleep. They are unconsciously falling through the cracks in the system; fading into the traps of the system.

The system was not thought of the way it is by design. It just turned out to be such and since it works for a powerful minority it has been allowed to run that way. But enough is enough and it can no longer continue to be. Humanity has been stagnant for very long a period and the evolution of everyone is at stake.

The mass population, the Intellectual Collective, needs to be consciously awakened to an evolved education system. Surely enough after their brains start being fed proper knowledge, personal evolution will ensue its due course.

If institutional reconfiguration is key in the process of elevating humanity out of starvation, homelessness, sickness and ignorance, equally true is the accurate and timely allocation of currency.

It is said that currency has taken many names and shapes throughout history. Early man would barter goods they had in surplus for ones they lacked. Cacao is said to have been the payment method for a day's work in ancient times. And several other stories of types of currency are found as one reads into past centuries.

A currency that has found inclusion in the entire world today is illegal drugs. Most countries lack to officially acknowledge it, but officials in high places know it is an undeniable fact. It is sought out by the world's population to numb their consciousness in lieu of living its unfulfilled reality.

Hollywood has made large investments taking to the big screen and television shows with movies made depicting the narcotics dealing business. It's a big eye opener. Everybody knows about it, but it takes an entire establishment to detain it effectively. Most mayor cities in the world have homeless people consuming dangerous substances on the streets; it's the method of choice to lose touch with the world they live in. Our book, now yours, lays the foundation for eradicating the use and abuse of hard drugs.

The sad lives that the dope consumers live is only comparable to the prison sentences carried out by the dealers each time they are caught. The current socioeconomic configuration of our system has proven ineffective because it continues to produce more of the same social problems.

It is time to replace the parts of our institutional layout that manufacture the wrong kind of currency. Not only is this wrongful manufacture creating a demand for its universal use, it is also forcing it into the bodies of the Intellectual Collective to be. Our teenagers, each year at an earlier age, are being introduced into the enslaving habit. It is the hour to remove the unfit components of our institutional disposition through adoption of the accessible-to-all, wealth-generating-methods, that we describe here.

There was a time when nobody was to be with blame for the outcome of the system in place up until this day. There is one acceptable excuse; the irrefutable truth that most of the implementations humanity activates are a product of trial and error due to the simple fact that humanity lacks knowledge of the future. People didn't have a crystal ball, two or three hundred years ago, to foresee the results of their executions. Now that we know, that which is to be kept and what is to be done away with, we must all be held responsible to do our part in fixing the wrongs. There no longer prevails excuse to delay taking immediate action. Everybody is in knowledge of the atrocity and now in this work we present the solution.

CHAPTER NINE

THE THIRD LEG

There's a portion of humanity that has had the right kind of fear, just in the correct amount, to spark enough intellect to dominate and propel a conscious, well measured and sensible outcome.

Very many intellectuals end up being institutionalized as a result of losing control of the amount of, and the quality of, the fuel that moves their engines. Mental rehabilitation institutions, correctional facilities, substance abuse clinics and many other organizations are full to the brim. It's a real pity because a lot of clock time goes to waste, vitality and physical energy going up in smoke.

Concomitantly, far too many intellectuals finish their days while still at a productive, young age. They become starved, homeless, ill or uneducated because not enough means of exchange is accessible to them. The proper amount of fuel and even maybe not the right fuel quality has been the motivation to move their engines.

And it seems that so is life. But it will be no more! Not as hopeless and fatalistic as it has been up to now. The remedy for solving humanity's basic needs is at hand.

Right from its beginning humanity was endowed with the ability to evolve, physically and intellectually, and it has and it will eternally continue to do so. The time is now; there is enough collective consciousness of the need for one another. Change is meant to happen.

The time is right and enough consciousness is ripe. That third leg of the human tripod, that third portion of humanity that is fearful enough just in the right amount and quality, is moving its engines to create balance among the two other legs and among ourselves to right the wrongs.

CHAPTER TEN

SELF LOVE

We often identify with loving our parents and children, our siblings and partners, more than we do identify with loving ourselves. More often than not we establish relationships with them and not often enough do we establish loving relationships with ourselves.

Loving the self is not as natural as it ought to be. Close your eyes for ten seconds and try visualizing the face of somebody familiar to you; your best friend for example. Close your eyes a second time and try visualizing your own face now; it's not as simple. Is it?

In our minds we can picture the faces of our relatives much easier than we do our own and that's because we see them more often than we look at ourselves in the mirror. That makes us more in love with them than with ourselves. Our concern for their welfare is greater and more latent than that of our own. Up in my head I can picture my brother and my sister playing checkers; I can clearly see the gestures on their faces. Yet I can't see myself, just as clearly, making the same faces.

Very seldom times do we have a mirror in front of us when we perform our daily routine. Go on people, start attending indoor activities in which the walls are 360 degrees covered with mirrors. Participate at gyms with mirrors, at dance classes with a full body view of yourself. Allow your eyes to fall in love with the image of you.

Having the resemblance of the loved one makes it much easier to keep the love alive. But, since we don't constantly see ourselves we're not as aware of the love for ourselves. Has it ever happened to you that you listen to a recording of your own voice during a speech or event and you're not familiar with the sound of your own pitch? Yet you listen to somebody speak in another room or different part of the house and immediately you recognize them just by the sound of their voice. Amazing relationship! Isn't it?

Life threatening situations are sometimes the necessary force that threaten us into contacting with our own physical selves. Having to care for a wound or physical injury reminds us that we have only one of us in this material existence. But then, something occurs to a loved one and again we forget about ourselves. That's a very irresponsible thing to do. You're in charge of yourself and whatever happens to you, you're to be held accountable for. Never forget your primary responsibility.

Not only is it possible to care for ourselves while in the care of others, but it is the wise thing to do. It is impossible to extend something one does not possess. When you don't have the conscious inclination of self, anything done for others is an automatic instinctual reaction. Conscious love for the self is the only love worth sharing with others. Love thy neighbor as it were yourself begins with loving thy self to love thy neighbor.

Loving our neighbors is sometimes as difficult as loving ourselves. We care so much for them until we realize they are in a squabble with our next of kin. Right away we become biased and choose sides. So, how much did we really love them?

If the situation between our brother and our neighbor escalates, then we want revenge. We want to take matters into our own hands. So again, how much love did we really have for our neighbor? And even worse, how much love do we have for ourselves when we take matters into our own hands? Should we risk being excessive? Committing an atrocity and then facing the consequences? Were we then really conscious of loving ourselves? Probably not.

Love is grand! Love is unconditional and it sure isn't biased. Real love starts with the consciousness of the self. No other person in this Universe of persons is yourself. You have been granted total uniqueness and so have they and everyone else. Look into a mirror and see how perfect your imperfections are and realize in your conscious mind that there are other people that love you just because of who you are.

Wake up to loving yourself. Grow the love for yourself to the point where you have enough real conscious love to flow over to your next of kin. Reflect again and go back to the consciousness of continuing to grow love for yourself until some more of your love can flow over to your next of kin and from there to your neighbor and to the rest of the persons of the universe. In this sense you'll always have so much love for yourself that consciousness of self will never leave you again. And then real love will flow from you and back to you.

Each Conscious Intellectual Individual is a Universe in the making within themselves. A raw creation with the ability and responsibility to continue to build upon themselves the eternal and endless progression to perfection that even nature is still building upon and will eternally continue to do so.

CHAPTER ELEVEN

A DIFFERENT FABRIC....ONE UNIQUE BLEND

From a mass of gas and clashing meteorites and acid rains, nature has evolved to a point of hosting our human kind. It has evolved its water streams to such suitable perfection that it is good enough to allow for human consumption.

Is nature alive? Does it have the free will to evolve? Has nature risen to the consciousness of prioritizing the needs of humanity? Has nature been evolving from its tumultuous origins to becoming the providing mother that it is today?

Nature provides equally for all, it does not discriminate among any. We: conscious humanity, the third leg of the human tripod, are the intellectual limbs of nature. We are the ones that can allow for the wealth of nature to reach each one of its inheritors. It is only consciousness that differentiates us from one another.

Aren't we, the third leg of the human tripod, that have to step up to bat and pinch in our contribution of Intellectual Consciousness in the accessibility process of the basic threshold every human being is entitled to, namely Food, Shelter, Health and Education?

It is only obvious that all humans were not naturally equipped to perform the same tasks in the evolution of our kind. A numbered few are very talented and multitaskers but the fact is most are not. Most excel in one particular field. A seasoned painter has a set of talents and the calling to draw beautiful landscapes. The farmer learns skills that drive him to making the land fertile. Although they both may enjoy art, both most certainly need food, shelter, healthcare and education.

The engineer and the brick setter are no different in relation to their basic needs. Neither is any different the truck driver from the forklift operator when it comes to their basic needs. Ask Pedro, the great, if he could have pitched at 100 MPH without his basic needs met. The important thing is that no matter who you are in life, you are a member of Team Humanity. The only prerequisite is to be conceived. You make it to 120? Great! Team Humanity has your back.

Those of us in the third tripod echelon are the ones called to perform change. Including the ones that hold the current structure in place. Disallow the monotony that keeps you in the emptiness of your current status; approve growth and transformation of yourself by being active in elevating humanity. We are beyond having our basic needs met and can give back in order to continue growing in the food chain.

The ceiling has to be busted in order to reach for the limitless sky. Remember that it doesn't matter where you're at, the sky is always up. We can always continue growing once the ceiling is busted. But at this point the weight of those at the bottom is so heavy that our ascension is no longer possible.

Humanity has exhausted all its growing potential with its current fuel. Every Intellectual at the bottom must join the good fuel production in order for us all to be able to pick up growing momentum again. That can only happen if we on top loosen up the bottle neck limiting the unity between the top and the bottom.

It's either that or pressure buildup will cause the bottle to burst by its narrow neck and gravity will push everybody to the bottom. Gravity never pushes upward, only consciousness can outturn the desired results in an upward motion

CHAPTER TWELVE

PURPOSE OF THE INSTITUTIONS

The evolution of the intellect has been very generous to humankind. Although the greatest scientists say that humanity as a whole is only in charge of a one digit percentage of its brainpower capabilities, it has traversed enough in its understanding to allow it to make of nature a truly beneficial partner. The human processor is capable of deciphering many of the components that make up the rest of creation and put it to good use.

The Intellectual Collective is ready to make sensible use of its material resources. All of these material gifts in one way or another derive from the abundance of the earth and its atmosphere.

Mostly through trial and error humanity has been sorting all of its activities into different categories. Each of these categories accordingly generate a body of regulations to which those individuals participating therein abide by. Such organization of activities has led to the formation of institutions and the institutions have preceded the establishments that govern each nation.

The Intellectual Collective having continuously evolved to greater consciousness is now more than ready to reap the fruit of its organization. The intellectual collective has acknowledged the constitution of great institutions. Starting with its own Self, the Intellectual Collective has established family, neighbors, communities of neighbors, associations and many other institutions.

Many years ago the individual survived taking from the land, without much effort, the things they needed for their simple lives. They would collect wild fruits and vegetables and quench their thirst belly down on a stream of water. Their need for clothing and shelter was also provided directly by the land.

Primitive people didn't have much work assigned to them, but they were prone to action so they would roam about until they felt the need for food. They stopped and gathered fruits from the trees in their surroundings. Since the unconscious intellect was already forging an economic driven individual, after they had filled their stomachs and taken a nap, they would collect some more to continue on with their journey.

Already they were gathering provisions to keep themselves going when they were to be traveling through unknown territories; in other words they were saving for later. They knew it was only a matter of time before they would need to replenish their energies.

Humanity has evolved plenty since its beginnings. Today we speak of an Intellectual Collective that reunites in big buildings for work and joy, to pray and debate. Many activities are conducted outdoors in the view of beautiful landscapes shaped by human hands and many other naturally created ones.

Today's individual is advanced in so many aspects that it's not even comparable to its predecessor. Today's human is an institution themselves, a much more conscious one.

The human person has needs that are born from within the matter of its constitution. Need for activity and need to rest. Consequently energy consumption and the call for nourishment. Digestive activities compromise the body within and out. The need to bathe and comfort. The need for shoes and clothing. The need of protection from the elements and the environment. The call for mating and reproduction.

The corporeal economy has organs that are stationary within the human body, therefore the call for physical activity and proper nutrition. The heart, the lungs, the liver and the spleen, just to name a few, have internal activity within themselves but not for themselves. Consequently, the outer limbs of the human body must perform periodic activity in order to maintain healthy blood flow to those organs and keep them healthy so they can in turn maintain the overall health of the corporeal economy.

It is important to recall some of those basic internal physical human working systems for the purpose of making the necessary analogies. Analogies as to how the intellectual collective needs its institutions to cooperate among each other as a coordinated system in order to maintain the proper stability required by the individual.

Every human made system is often an extension or an analogy of the grandiose creation of the human.

A recreation of its own physical constitution and physiology. All of nature is creation, including humanity, and both nature and humanity evolve out of its basic origin.

Eventually we must make our creative evolution work hand in hand from core to limbs just as all of nature does. The Institutions we have so ardently eventuated and systematized must return their benefits to us whom are its authors and co-creators. To us that have spent our time and energy refining its functionality.

Why co-create the marketplace, ever so large and efficient if not for the benefit and wellbeing of the marketplace co-creators? Why co-create the banking institution, ever so powerful and rich if not for the enrichment of the communities and marketplace duelers that co-created it? Why co-create the establishment of government, ever so expensive if not for guaranteeing the basic needs of the Intellectual Collective that put it in place?

Now as we know... the human body is much more than matter and physical activities. It is also comprised of sensations, sentiments and emotions.

All these feelings when activated by a proper or improper physical activity, whether voluntary or by involuntary cerebral command, trigger in turn an otherwise dormant psyche. Heck! The human composition is much more than this. But this gives us a glimpse of, when the analogy is considered, how much more involved in the welfare of the individual must our institutions be.

The abundance of the earth is selective. It is not all situated in the same place. Imagine that it all were found in the same location, we would have enormous uninhabited portions of the earth. In certain regions we'll find wood for structuring a house, in another roofing material is found. That's the origin of private property and of different countries with their diverse cultures and borders. That is the reason explaining the establishment of the market place and of trading among one same people and among different races. It was all conceived in that manner at origin.

Diamonds, gold, silver, copper, zinc, iron, nickel, bauxite, amber, soap trees, petroleum, natural gas, lumber trees, fertile soil, rocks, mountains, seas, drinking water, tropical forests, and even beautiful flowers, all happen and are naturally situated in different regions. Aside from dawn and sunsets they all happen and are naturally situated in different regions.

The individual collective of one region has needs and wants for the goods in a region not readily accessible to them. So, individuals would artificially recreate those things they wanted but did not have. Yet the real deal is always best and desirable.

In such a design, when the European landed in America and the indigenous races of the new world realized that they could recreate their own image by use of an artifact called the mirror, the native Tainos were ready to trade their shiny rocks for the pleasure found in the satisfaction of their vanity. Wow! They fell in love with their own image. And it was cool! For the first time in their lives they were in front of themselves. Both parties, the conquerors with their shiny rocks and the conquered with their mirrors, were happy. In such a sense America learned that knowledge is a great capital, and it still is today. So let's beat ignorance by boosting education to the heights necessary so that everyone can exhibit a similar threshold in general knowledge.

CHAPTER THIRTEEN

THE COMMONALITY

Most known mammals mate and have offspring. In the animal kingdom the instinct compels the mother to care for their youngsters until a time when the new born has learned to take care of itself and then the parental responsibility is over.

The conscious human looks after their baby forever. A deep bond of love develops and is never broken. The parents will look after their children throughout the developing stages and beyond.

As adults the human sons and daughters engage into having children of their own while maintaining a loving relationship with their parents and the parents with their children's children. This goes on until there is no longer a consciousness of the relationship. The loss of consciousness of the familial relationship could be the result of senility, accident or some other illness.

Initially when the individual is still a single person, and as the journey goes on, they would store food for their own consumption. But, when the person has a family they will be collecting and storing food for all the members of their family unit. And later, they would also procure protection for every member of their family pack. Protection from the elements, the environment and from predators.

Part of those individuals were really engaged in their security and that of their family. They roamed about until they found a fertile piece of land near a stream of water. They would then claim said territory as their own and made it productive.

This was their means of providing food and shelter for themselves and their dependents. In this fashion, and as long as they worked the land, they provided for their present and for their future. The education consisted in handing down to their children the way to make the land fruitful. They were in control of their livelihood and weren't afraid of old age because they were able of making provision for it. The children would make sure their aged parents were taken care of in the same manner the parents had looked after them in the days of their infancy. That was real and guaranteed life insurance.

Having stability was really simple because there was more land to work and live upon than there was people to oppose such actions. Nonetheless there were those that even though caring for themselves and their family continued to live off the land and moved around wherever food and shelter was to be found. And that was acceptable; everyone had the opportunity to choose how to go about their lives.

Those families with adjoining properties became neighbors. In this mode of living, communities where established. Their communities had meaning; they shared some interests in common. And most times it was a stream of water.

Larger water streams provided for the formation of larger communities. Adjoining families would exchange their abundance for things that they lacked.

When larger communities wanted to trade they would put up a meeting point where all the neighbors would bring their surpluses in exchange for their needs. In this fashion the marketplace was born and now the community had more than just the water stream in common.

At that point in time not only did the human person care for themselves and their family but also for their neighbors and the things that they had in common.

As those communities grew bigger in number and extension, individuals sharing the same water streams and market place got together to set regulations for the better use and preservation of their commonalities.

Cattle herders could only water their animals downstream from the men's bathing area. For example, women and children bathing area only. No herd crossing allowed upstream of the drinking water spring. Certain members of the "Water Stream Preservation Group" would enforce and maintain these regulations.

The Marketplace Group would ensure that only the healthiest crop was brought for exchange. They would also make sure everyone's exhibit place was left tidy and clean at the end of the day, etc., etc.

Even bigger communities would have associations according to growers of a same crop. Others would specialize in seeding and crop collection. Others would be great at weeding and so forth.

Nature provided a wide variety of means for simple life support but humanity always strives for more and deserves more. Therefore, the intellectual collective was creating expansion and comfortability, and more associations were put in place.

Some of those associations became institutions that still today regulate and define the way the human collective lives in comfort or not.

Let's not forget about those that continued to live off the land without settling down to a piece of property. They automatically became denominated as the ones that remained outside of an association. They were not known to be a part of any of the established communities.

They weren't a part of any of the existing neighborhoods and certainly not part of any of the established families.

They played with chance and luck and further down the road of human evolution many of them would become the salaried laborer of the property owners.

For the time being their basic needs were met because there were more unclaimed territories than not. It was only a limited portion of land that one man and his family could tend to. The earth and its atmosphere still provided for the wanderers, but they lacked the strength of the institutions.

CHAPTER FOURTEEN

A FAVORABLE OPTION

Some chose to settle and have institutions while others stayed living a nomadic existence. The Creator of life, or creators of life as one may choose to believe, allowed for a free will evolution in mortal existence.

As time passed and institutions led to governments and larger governments led to the so called Establishment... well, guess what! The Establishment took on a life of its own! Whatever land was not of private property became the property of the establishment.

At this point the nomad was cornered. Ouch! Where would they roam and live now? Even if the migrant decided to settle down now, there was no land left for them to call-it their own.

Since humanity is lacking much of the facts in many aspects of its origin, we can only read the signs left behind by earlier civilizations and speculate as to how we arrived at our current state of affairs.

When factual knowledge is unavailable, popular belief is a notion to fall back unto. Curiosity comes forth from the dark and sometimes allows for insight into the unknown past. Curiosity brings along a hunch of reality, but because our human lives are so ephemeral we can only rely on our beliefs.

In the vast mentality of Creation, co-Creation was definitely part of the scheme. Intellectual human beings endowed with the ability to evolve must be able to at some point be capable of giving back. Not so much as giving back, but sharing back and being magnanimous. Making the right choice definitely allows for institutional support.

Evolution as a calling urged humanity to create educational institutions. The educated ones have the right to take the itinerant children and seat them on their laps; out of compassion impart knowledge, so that they also can make the right choice in life and attain institutional support.

Co-creating is not a choice to make; co-creating is a duty owed to those in lack. Everyone can co-create because there is always good to be done for someone in a more fragile state of being. Simply put, everyone co-creates, but all are not conscious of it.

A bit at a time, more and more humans will be wise enough to make a choice from wisdom. All thanks to the magnanimous ones. The ones that once upon a time took upon the correct option of congregating into a community for hard work and productivity. The kindness of wisdom allows for much more good to be recognized unto humanity. The best part of it is that there is always the free will and the opportunity to convene on doing the proper thing.

Those that chose to settle down for the sake of looking after their families in matters of nutrition, with a health objective in mind; for the purpose of physical protection or simply to acquire distinction, to elevate their sense of pride; just seeking for better opportunities, and in every kind of way imaginable to humanity; by chance or consequence set the foundation for the institutions that are in place today.

Long before the actual banking institutions were established, humanity would bury their treasures for safekeeping from bandits.

Making a withdrawal was more like grabbing a shovel to unearth their vault, grab as much of the treasure needed to exchange for whatever good they were trying to acquire and all while looking over their shoulder.

They needed to play it safe and be certain that no one was watching them. Same deal if they were trying to make a deposit, almost like today, but hiding in the bushes. There was never a problem if they were careful enough.

Particularly, buried treasures were more a burden than a blessing. The owner knew they possessed one, but what good was it? They couldn't boast about it or even tell a friend for the fright of losing it. Even worse if by chance a rain storm or an animal or some other fiat of nature erased the mark that identified the location of it.

Thanks to fear and intellect for the creation of banks. Among the most important institutions in the world economy are banks. We can't delay spreading the private banking institution to a broader radius of action. We owe to the banking industry that the hardworking and wise decision makers, the generous and prosperous intellectual individuals, don't have to fear losing their fortunes at the hands of outlaws. An added benefit to the banking institution is that since its creation it is possible to show-off your wealth. Wearing nice clothing and driving your new car down the street while your money is safe in a bank vault is totally sane.

Because of the marvelous creation of the banking institution the Intellectual Collective is on a confident journey to a great future. The banking institution is the platform that shall promote the true definition of an enhanced society of all people in the world. Banks are the central springboard that will flex to the ground propelling the economy to great heights.

CHAPTER FIFTEEN

GLOBALIZATION

Globalization is not as new a concept as our generation of thinkers has been reared to visualizing since the final years of the past century. Humanity has always perceived the world as the lands described in the cartography of the times. Knowledge of geography has always been closely linked to the means of transportation and telecommunication available to science. Modern satellites are aiding immensely in the job of scrutinizing the planet. We have a long way to go in searching the ocean floors and the depth of the earth.

The discovery of a new land and its people has always caused awe among the commonalty and been possible according to the technology at hand. According to the technology in use at this time we have dominion of the entire world and its properties until a new implementation debunks truths and beliefs.

As a human conglomerate watched how a tree fell out of its old roots and started rolling downhill towards them, many ran for cover. But, there was always one or two that were brave and curious enough to stand out of the way while watching it roll past them.

Thrilled and amused as they were, there was that one intellectual that realized that by slicing it into chunks, they would develop a rolling piece of tree which they later refined into the invention of the wheel. And then in time another intellectual or probably the same person realized that by connecting two wheels with a straight tree branch they would invent a cartwheel.

As time went by, a four wheel wagon was aiding these intellectuals with the transportation of their tools and materials to farther places a lot easier. By the fantastic invention of the wheel their world became a lot smaller because they could cover much more land much faster.

The intellectual collective started having consciousness of the realization of their thoughts and imaginations. At such a moment humanity started evolving at a much faster rate because of a spark of consciousness that had been ignited in the intellect.

The intellectuals got on their wagon and soon they were building bridges to take their new invention across rivers. Those weren't the same intellectuals from past ages. Those intellectuals were putting a horse in front of a wagon and later two and three horses. Later they realized how much faster they could go, how much farther they could go, if only they had a horse that wouldn't get tired as soon.

This civilization is not young when one looks at it from a human perspective. And yet only less than one hundred and thirty years ago did this humanity defeat the invention of the wheel and began air hopping. Only less than one hundred years ago was the first computer made. And only less than thirty years ago was the World Wide Web invented.

As humanity has expanded out of its mindset of unity into greater disparity it has crafted considerable greatness of the outer institutions conforming The Establishment. The Establishment has gotten away with forgetting the basic, inner and original foundation that has given greatness and fortitude to it all, THE CONSCIOUS HUMAN INSTITUTION.

By expansion and globalization of certain cultural values, ethnic and moral worth have been thinly spread and the strength in knowing your neighbor, your community and society has weakened.

The institutional structure has lost much of its appreciation for the collective under guise of anonymity. We no longer know those in charge in our institutions and they do not know who their position in society is subject to. Reason being they have started serving themselves and forgotten their sacred duty to the people.

Smoke signal was probably the first technology precursor of globalization. The idea was to stay within reach by transmitting a message across a great distance in an almost instantaneous fashion. First the canoe and then the wheel continued making the physical connection of greater distances but at a much slower rate.

The ship and the airplane covered greater distances but the telegraph transmitted a faster and more precise message. The real enhancer of the telecommunications was the telephone. The telephone was really quick and the transfer of voice made it unbeatable. But the telephone as the telegraph channeled a signal that was encased in a wire. Where there wasn't access to the wire, telecommunication signals could not be dispatched

CHAPTER SIXTEEN

HUMAN PRIORITIZATION

In a previous chapter we mentioned that business transactions where conducted by the direct exchange of goods between individuals in a well instituted marketplace. Prioritizing in order of importance we should arrive upon the following sequence: Individual persons/farmers processing/growing commercial/ edibles goods/ which are products that change hands in the marketplace institution.

The previous sequence can be simplified as follows: Individual farmers growing and groups of persons processing commercial edible goods which are products that change hands in the marketplace institution.

The institution has been constituted following the guidelines of a lawful regulation that governs its functionality. Laws that are formulated by the starring individuals and whom are willing to abide by said laws.

The institution in this particular scenario is the marketplace, but it applies to any and all practices. The Marketplace organization has been erected for the welfare of the basic and original foundation which we have previously called "THE CONSCIOUS HUMAN INSTITUTION. So by simple definition, The Marketplace is to serve the best interests of the Intellectual Collective.

It definitely was not built with the vice versa purpose in mind. Science must always be at the service of humanity, and not vice versa. Shamefully the establishment has come to believe that it deserves to be praised in detriment of the Intellectual Collective.

As we have built along on the institutional scale, we mentioned a body of law that governed the marketplace. One such law could have been, let's say for the sake of argument, that initially: in order to have a spot for selling goods at the marketplace center an individual had to be a member of one of the families. One of the families that had settled down and claimed a piece of land with the intention of making it continuously productive. And of course, to prosper from the yield of their labor.

As the communities became more and more numerous, also various types of markets were being founded. Not only farmers markets, but artisanal markets as well, livestock markets and butcheries; this and that market, and that other thing market; etcetera, etc. At which point there was an interaction among different markets and their constituents.

In the meantime, the different market activities added their own laws and regulations. Pretty soon the institution of law came into play.

By this time the nomadic people had become artists and inventors giving birth to the Intellectual Property. Remember that they had kept themselves out of the private property ownership scheme.

The nomads had invented musical instruments and learned how to play them. They enacted plays, they sang and danced. They learned magic tricks and entertained, thus creating the entertainment industries.

Somebody gave it enough thought and soon enough getting sick was invented; the healing and shamanic chores also sprung into activity. The ball was rolling.

All of the above activities and many others have become standardized and industrialized, but not so much the welfare of "THE CONSCIOUS HUMAN", the Intellectual Collective. And we don't see why not.

The closest thing to the well-being of the collective is the handout certain establishments extend to their population. In order to qualify the individual must be down and out and staying down. It is made certain that the rest of the population, those not receiving welfare benefits, looks down on the recipients of the social charity. Totally undesirable.

All the pertaining institutions are already in place and the intention of creating the standards for the welfare of humanity is alive and kicking. What do we need to do to give everyone access to a fair start out of the basic-core needs of the Intellectual Collective? It's so simple that it's ludicrous that no one has proposed the solution to such unacceptable omission.

While not being overly crass for our procrastinating selves, people have to command the responsibility for our own wellbeing. Just as the Intellectual Collective toiled for ages carrying heavy loads on their back and one bright, sunshiny day the wheel was invented, in that same line of thought, who is to say that humanity isn't about to rejoice because the heavy burden of inequality of opportunities is now being lifted off its shoulders.

CHAPTER SEVENTEEN

REVOLUTION OF THE ECONOMY

Back in the day of the marketplace storyline when the first human communities occurred, people worked for food and shelter. No matter how hard they worked all there was to show was more of the same. More land and crops, cattle and children.

At about the same time that curiosity and vanity and pride started motivating people to look different, and dressing and living differently, certain nomads picked up trades: hair fashioning and tailoring, and jewelry making; they too started to settle down.

Nomads were able to develop talents that allowed them to serve the incipient communities with a profession of their own. Here it is made evident that the Intellectual individual is an institution in themselves: nobody has been known to purchase a diaphragm to begin a career as a singer. Talents are discovered much like America was first discovered by Christopher Columbus. He came up to nothing while he was sitting in the Queen's living rooms. It was when he decided to set sail, and actually do it, when he eventually came upon dry land. He discovered land new to his eyes. Nobody is born devoid of a treasure. Look long enough within yourself and you'll discover more of you.

As soon as the Intellectual Individual realizes the needs and opportunities of their immediate environment, their latent talents begin emerging. Enabling them to become self-sufficient, and an aid to their fellow citizen.

Every human has the seed of greatness in them. Their godlike qualities are ever present in their unconscious psyche awaiting for a beam of light to awaken them from their lethargy. This is the imperative reason why the well-established institutions are now called to become conscious of their functioning. Institutions are living entities of which we are the moving limbs; they also need to evolve from time to time. At this point in time such changes are necessary in order to afford every human the opportune threshold to evolve into their higher selves. A higher self that in short becomes the stepping stone for others trailing behind to become more and more aware of their duty and free will to evolve.

This economy would not be trading hairstyling for watermelons much longer. The direct exchange could no longer satisfy the needs and wants of the evolving economy. A more dynamic valve had to be let open for the welcoming and better appreciation of more commodities. Services were being offered in addition to the traditional products on the market.

The economy was bursting out of its bubble. A common unit of value that would be of interest to both the farmer and the nomad, the artist and the craftsman, had to be found. And once the banking institution was established this would be much easier to decide upon than ever before.

Anyone and everyone keeping their treasures in the bank, namely gold, was issued a bank note. A note legal tender for all debts public and private in the amount of its gold equivalent. Ordinary people that had no treasures to keep in the bank hired their idle hands in exchange for bank notes.

The natural course of business included that those bank notes were to be redeemed at the bank, of course, in exchange for gold. Most people kept the gold deposited in the bank and the notes continued changing hands.

Evidently, the real material wealth was in the banks. Thus, banks prospered because now they were able to trade based on a commodity that was not their own. Bankers charged the depositors in order to keep their wealth in a secure vault. If for any reason the proprietors became forgetful they could lose a chunk of their monies through bank deductions and other loopholes among interest fees.

Bankers lobbied to have laws enacted that protected them from having to return the totality of your treasures at any given time. Do you see how it works? This is how institutions become entities, alive, and are able to acquire immunity in their business activities. Is this wrong? This is where it gets tricky, but it has a simple solution. This is the part where education plays a starring role and rearranging the relationship between the establishment, the institutions and the rightful owners of the economy is relevant.

What is not correct is the way the proceeds of doing business in such a fashion are distributed in a

straightjacket   Establishment   ruling-only
atmosphere.

Banks in the business model that we're signaling here are not to be called lending institutions, but some form of currency revolving institutions instead. This is when the evolution becomes severely dynamic and profitable.

Their functioning will consist in the capturing and allocation of capital. Not much different from now, but instead of retribution of a low single digit profit margin to the rightful owner, a larger amount should be returned.

The revolving institution, in this case the bank, should receive a single digit profit because the large volume of transactions that it will be conducting in this new business model will allow it to amass greater benefits. The ratio and activities can be altered in this new model because the benefits of the banking institution and that of the people and the taxes collected for government will all be very much enhanced and augmented.

We have already established that the individual is the primary institution. In doing business people are to be dealt with as the integral institution that we already are; the arrow head institution. Every other institution in the Establishment is enacted by people and lead by people.

The law that is now needed is one allowing the banking institution to allocate in the local community the necessary funds. Funds necessary to activate the local production and promotion of food, shelter, health and education, as a primary investment. All other business activities will be addressed according to community priorities.

The only reason depriving many children in developed countries, such as The United States of America, from having access to the school bus is because it is mainly a State funded program.

No State in any part of the world will be capable of providing services in a universal manner. The only satisfactory provision for a service that is universally required is to pay for it. The only guarantee for a good service is to pay top currency for it. The only guarantee for a good school is to pay big currency to the teachers.

The basic guarantee you and we need from the Establishment is total accessibility to the factorization of our talents.

Now that we have only mentioned a developed country, The USA in our last example. In this sensitive issue of providing a basic universal service such as the school bus for students, let's address the third world.

Staying in the Western Hemisphere, not to wander far away, let's move south to The Hispaniola. Let's make a Caribbean sun stop in The Dominican Republic. Let's ask ourselves how efficient could this third world country be in addressing a State funded service such as the one we just mentioned. Be it known that The Dominican Republic does not have a public school bus system in place for its population of students.

Will The Dominicans ever meet a satisfactory standard providing such a service as the school bus for every student in our current state of affairs? Not in a million years. The current status quo is maxed out. Third world countries will forever be third world countries in the current state of our institutional layout. They will forever be dependents of the civilized world as we know it. Waiting for a meager handout is the foreseeable destiny. Wake up world! Come back to developing greatness! It is expected of us. We will, sooner or later, and now is the calling. Now is the time.

By the time the economy was being weighed in gold many changes had occurred in the evolution of the Conscious Human. No longer did mankind live freely off the land. The land now belonged to the State, the Church or was privately owned.

Churches and the State have thought that promoting the idea of giving charity to the Collective was a Godly thing to do. Nothing more crippling than creating a beggar out of a God-resembling creature. They could never be more wrong.

The Intellectual Collective needs not the handouts collected from such institutions. The Intellectual Collective craves education and the opportunity to thrive and provide for their own needs. How much pride is derived from getting in line to receive less than one deserves? And that's if there's anything left when reaching the front of the line. Risible? It is not.

Let's move farther West on the same Hispaniola Island towards the people of Haiti. By the way, as a point of information, The Hispaniola is one of a limited number of islands that conserves more than one independent nations.

The Republic of Haiti, only second to the United States in obtaining independence in all of the Americas, really needs a hand in rebuilding its institutions and an initial push in the implementation of them. Haiti cannot and should not have to eternally depend on the foundations that are bringing an aid that is never enough. The one thing that the determined people of the free will nation of Haiti need is its institutions transformed to functioning to the likes described in these chapters.

Probably the great international minds looking to fill their hands with the treasures buried in the Haitian mountains would be willing to organize a strong banking institution that will allow the formation of a wealthy nation.

Sovereign Dominican Republic hasn't had great luck with its Establishment and its institutions. Filled mostly with unprofessional and deceiving politicians, as is most of Latin America. Public servants that collude in illegal drugs trafficking, setting a terrible precedent for the starved, homeless, sickly and ignorant to follow into.

Dominicans also have had to migrate illegally throughout its history in the search of opportunities into nations with stronger institutions. That should never happen when its institutions become rearranged to serve the Intellectual Collective instead of its large Establishment.

Such a paradise in the Caribbean Sea! A beautiful country with tons of natural resources and yet a clear and true example of a terribly bad institutional grouping. The Dominican people is an entrepreneurial race. Excellent farmers with abundant farmlands and a great host for its tourists and visitors. But, the Establishment is greedy and its institutions do not function for the benefit of the Intellectual Collective.

Those that did not own property nor had developed their latent talent continued wandering in what is now called the public way and became down-and-out. They have become confused in a world that continues changing while they have not found the right track to fall into. Feeling alone and different is how they find themselves.

Progress has always been good and is what is expected of humanity. Private property has propelled the world to great heights. Private property brings distinction and brilliance to the tenacious hard workers, to the curious inventors and the proud achievers in surpassing their own goals.

Taxes collected from private property ownership has to allow for the betterment and advancement of the great mass of impoverished since being left out of their natural habitat. The confusion and chaos that has invaded the lives of the famished is now being felt by the honorable taxpayers. Those law abiding citizens are also victims of crime and lawlessness resulting from the great disadvantage at play in many areas of social life.

Accessibility is the necessary incentive for a healthy economy competing to increase itself. Each Conscious Human competing with oneself to make their own economy greater and greater. Not needing to worry about disparity and the results thereof. That is the competition every healthy economy in the world wants to sustain within its confines.

Instead of having an obnoxious administration of the Intellectual Collective's Economic Means, the State should serve as a regulator in the allocation of currency. The State is to be a responsible supervisor of the banking institution in its relationship with the Intellectual Collective and a better negotiator of the surpluses in national production.

The State has demonstrated to be the great opportunist in the endeavors of tax collection. Stop taxing the production of goods and services and the costs of producing them. Apply a simple tax collection only to the benefits resulting from the trade of said goods and services. In today's technologically advanced world all we need is a community bank in every commonwealth.

Every cost and expense incurred in the production of goods and services, and in the trading transaction of those goods and services, can and should be totally recorded through the community bank.

Currency should be equivalent to a number amount in a bank account. Very little paper money is needed in pocket. This day and age everybody and their children owns a smartphone. Combine a smartphone and a currency card and you own the means of exchange necessary for any money transaction anywhere within national borders.

In abundantly rich countries with economically deprived citizens such as The Central African Republic, Venezuela; Haiti and Dominican Republic, just to name a few; this system is to be implemented yesterday!

Let's not forget that the people isn't and shouldn't be taxed. It is the yields of the capitals that should pay taxes because the means of exchange, the currency, is a national Symbol administered by the State. It is from the interest gained that tax is to be deducted.

Being that money is a state symbol in the hands of the people for the promotion of personal wealth, than in gaining affluence, it is only fair that the people pay a tax to the State. The public does not have the means to manufacture legal tender notes and there is a cost associated with the production of cash. Therefore it is expected that a benefit be associated to its use.

Why not allocate plenty currency to every possible capital multiplier. Of course! Strong supervision and responsible counseling must accompany such allocations. Only the private banking system should run the day to day economy.

A public banking system should exist to manage data pertaining to the world economy and to advise its nationals accordingly. Other obligations include supervision of the private banking system and the satisfaction of the private sector with enough currency to run the economy.

The government, in matters of monies, would only be another customer of the private banking system. The Public Banking System should run parallel to government and not subordinated to it. Each institution supervising that the other is doing their job.

It is for a good reason that the accountant that registers the transactions in a company does not sign the checks. The individuals charged with signing the checks cannot modify or make any entries in the registry books; those reasons are all related to safe keeping of the capitals and the separation of powers.

In such a national structure, government and the public banking system work in unison and parallel in function to each other. Both systems exchange information with the Electoral College via appointees of said organism working directly in both the public banks and the Presidency. The Electoral College is to be in constant coordination with the congress of community members of each local community.

The private banking system is the liaison institution in the matters pertaining to currency between the congress of community members and both government and public banking. The private banking system alike the public and government include appointees hailing from The Electoral College. Only the private banks allocate cash and vault the proceeds from the collection of taxes.

The private banking system is the only institution entitled to extend payment to any and all other institutions in matters pertaining to salaries earned by workers and expenses incurred in running said institutions. The government institutions and its employees are not to be exempt from this measure.

The institutions under the umbrella of government may write checks or process a direct deposit to its employees, but it is the private banks that do the actual check cashing or take the deposits. The public institutions would already have access to the monies from tax collection that the government vaults in the private banks. In this sense, government can never be larger than the money it collects nor write more checks than the monies deposited because they keep their books but never the people's money.

CHAPTER EIGHTEEN

STABILITY

When the gross domestic product grew in unison with the world population and its modern demands, the amount of gold in the vaults could not keep up with the new increase without shrinking the economy. Thus each national economy decided to allocate enough currency to satisfy the supply of products and services being demanded by a larger population.

Such a way of allocating resources to comply with the expected needs of capital in the economy is an annual estimation which can never be close to accurate. It is never close to accurate because it is only partially funding the possible products to be grown or fabricated. Differently, allocations have to be made to every possible PRODUCER because not only growing and fabricating goods and services will be considered, but also eventuation of all kinds of goods and services can be accounted for. The current allocating system allows for big shortages or excesses of capital which are both opportunities for imbalances in the economy. Creating the wrong belief that the economy is run based on currency and not the actual production of goods and services. Which could be the difference between inflation and deflation versus economic stability.

When the bartering commerce was first modernized through the employ of an economy that was weighed in gold, the trading process became expedited and easier to keep track of. Shortly after, the increase in the production of goods and services outgrew the speed with which the precious metal was mined and the economy became restricted to the amount of gold at hand, which created inorganic emission of money.

A very creative way out was the anticipation of a Gross Domestic Product and the printing and allocation of currency to keep up with the production and consumption of goods.

What happened as a result of such estimations is that we created just as bad an evil. We started dealing with inflation and deflation. The economy became dependent on the accuracy of the estimation and the good management or not of such resources. There were periods of a booming in finances and times where there was a recession of the economy. We all know that during times of inflation many can't afford to meet their basic need requirements; during the epochs of recession is just as bad because there aren't enough goods to meet the demands of the people.

There is a major factor that became evident and that present day estimation of the economy has failed to address. The problem has become the disparity among being able to access currency, and the number of Intellectuals seeking an opportunity to become productive.

A head count of the population is indispensable when estimating both production of goods and adequate allocation of currency. To accurately provide for, and to achieve satisfaction of the basic needs demanded, the entire population has to be accounted for. All must have readily available access to currency and productivity. It is the organic process for stabilizing surpluses and lack; it is the equivalent to the natural bartering of goods without excluding the universal means of exchange.

The establishment will induce the Intellectual Collective to approach the community banking institution. The individual will want to retrieve, first and foremost financial advice, and consequently the necessary assets in a conjoint effort by the individual and the banking institution to make happen their success in creating personal wealth and productivity in the community.

Not all members in society will require the INSTITUTIONAL PUSH to retrieve their allotted monies, but counseling, advice and support should be mandatory to everyone.

Because of this mandate is that the banking institution will be ready to hire all sorts of professionals to stay abreast of productivity in the community.

No longer will the centrally located government be the one institution that mostly seeks professional and provides employment. In this newly created scheme the community will be its greatest competitor and in some countries the community might become a larger provider of quality employment vacancies. That is not the way that it is happening in most third world countries.

Once the goods and services become a manufacture reality the banking institution will have the professional marketers to assist the smaller and less knowledgeable newly graduated entrepreneurs.

With the banks functioning as the central engine of the economy, what follows is a well concatenated wealth producing nation. The former illegal immigrants that once invaded extra-national borders will be needed in order to grow their local economy. Lack of employment and productivity will be a thing of the past. Hunger, homelessness, disease and ignorance shall be automatically eradicated.

Every conceived and breathing person must be accounted for when allocating currency for the running year. Nutrition, shelter, health and education should be top priority when addressing the allocation of resources pertaining to each conceived and standalone breathing person in every stage of their biological existence.

If we recall, no longer does the Intellectual collective have a buried treasure to bank on. Everything money is to be mediated by the banks. The Banking Institution will be conducting business alongside the community and hiring all sorts of professionals, while collecting taxes from the money surpluses.

By partnering with the community members, banks and its professionals will be imparting a great deal of financial education to its communities. From the financial gains that both the communities and the banking institution generate, an amount will be redirected to pay the city's elected officials; including the congress of community members, and the member or members in the Electoral College. This means that while the community is supervising with their own eyes the presence of their incumbents and the work that they perform, government is being reduced in size and increased in efficiency.

This will generate a true tax collection apparatus and the government will receive an enormous amount of resources to bank on. The Intellectual Collective will be proud to contribute with a tax that's not burdensome to pay and render effective in matters of public works.

Cities will be retaining the best qualified minds and hands in the fields of safety and security for its citizens. Presidents will command the best armed forces and agencies that money can purchase. Both local and national departments will have great personnel to work with. And the basic needs of each and every citizen will be sourced and satisfied personally by each consumer.

Departments of defense all across the globe, from small to large nations, all get the needed attention their yearly budgets can give. The most critically important asset any nation can aspire to is its population.

The population is where allocation of funds is to begin and from there prioritize on everything else. The needs for nutrition, shelter, health and education has to be met and satisfied on a per capita basis. Everyone is to be accounted for.

The banking industry, born from private citizenry, should remain private. Those wealthy private citizens that entrusted their excess capitals to the banking industry, should remain the employers to bankers and be entitled to professional advice.

Most of the financial gains in the industry are not returning to its investors. In the same manner that the land was created for its dwellers, the gains of the land should be returning to its inhabitants in a fair and proportionate fashion.

That the gains of the land don't return to its inhabitants in a regulated fashion means that those that choose to work and make the land fruitful are entitled to their treasures in the process. And that their valuables should be multiplied with professional help and willing assistance from the banking system.

From the enhanced fortune created by sound counseling and management on the part of the banking professionals and regulated by a congress of private citizens, a portion should return to each of the participants in the form of a social responsibility.

Beneficiaries in the social responsibility process are the land and the environment. Included within the land and the environment is the crop from which the most adequate product should be kept for seeding. If the product is the result of a manufacture or an industrial process then social responsibility should restore the environment to its original state. The idea is to become universally responsible about the creation of wealth.

CHAPTER NINETEEN

MIGRATION AND STATE RESPONSIBILITY

Whether it be in the search for food, knowledge, adventure or simple curiosity the intellectual individual has always liked to go from place to place. Food and sustainment has always been a good motivator. History books have taught us that very early on, humans were totally nomad and probably not as aware of themselves as we are today. They would pillage the land and when there was no more food in a region they would move on and repeat their actions.

Even people with a history of zero motivation for activity, with the opportunity for traveling to another land could become engaged in productivity and exteriorize tremendous ability to perform. A lot of people travel to attend colleges and universities and many times they stay abroad and become residents of the new land. Foreign cultures are also attractions for many.

There are countries today that many centuries ago were plentiful in flora and fauna and due to bad farming procedures and soil erosion have become arid and unyielding. Yet, paradoxically enough a certain number of these same countries are rich in other natural resources such as minerals and precious metals or oil.

Totally perplexing is the fact that some of the poorest countries conforming the world map, possess a very abundant combination of several resources. One of the greatest obstacles that they come upon is the lack of equipment and technology to be able to exploit their wealth.

Would a transnational fair trade agreement play a role in alleviating the imbalance at play in certain regions of the world? Yes, absolutely. But alleviating the problem is not enough unless the next best step were to be death from starvation. Besides, most trade agreements cause a restriction of some sort on the economy of one of the participants or to more than one. Free enterprise has always been one of the key benefits of capitalism.

A World Bank type institution can finance and lend advice in the creation and installation of a banking system in the deprived regions of the world. Lending or selling capital and knowledge is a great promoter of the economy.

The needy regions of the world could very well take advantage in being financially and technologically aided in the creation of strong institutions. A jump start in the creation and installation of a solid banking industry with the aspects and functionality of the one described previously would greatly benefit both the poor country and the rest of the world.

The solution does not consist in lending the money and then leaving them to find out if they know what to do with it or not. The money is only part of the solution. The complete job entails coming in with the technology and personnel necessary to make the clock tick and gradually wean them off to their own people and resources.

The mission is to have a poor performance country up-and-running on their own as soon as possible. And consequently and responsibly collect the money owed plus due interests. Starting from the beginning of the operation, compromises should be adhered to by both the wealthy to be country and the bank.

Let's not forget the standard measure of a wealthy country. It is its Intellectual Collective. For as long as the people has not obtained access to currency and productivity such country is not wealthy. All legal issues regarding the installation of the new institutions are to have the guarantees of international law. Defaulting is inadmissible.

A poor country that creates access to its wealth is no longer poor. It strengthens the world economy in as much as it can insert its nationals into legal international trading activities.

Many third world countries are living below poverty lines and have become a burden to richer nations and their inhabitants. Criminal activities that begin in the impoverished states sooner or later migrate their troubles across neighboring borders creating a hemispheric instability and from there on to global imbalance.

It is widely known that institutions such as the International Monetary Funds have continuously come in aid of poor countries in facilitating financial tools. The owing nations continue to fall deeper and deeper into debt and only a handful have been able to repay and gain financial stability. Where is the problem? That only part of the solution was ever sought by the borrowing countries.

Many of such governments almost beg for the loans and then want to be left to their own sovereignty in dealing with the problem. The solution is hardly ever reached due to less than good faith in the administration of the funds. Many other times the restrictions imposed on the citizenry strangle the taxpayer's pockets; their plates become empty and they totally lose their livelihood.

The solution has to be received and given in its entirety or none at all. We're not seeking to alleviate a disorder, we're in the business of signaling for the cure of it. When all of the above is not embraced, never mind assuming the loans. Their national business consists in starving the people. Homelessness, health care issues and the lack of education are the least of their concerns.

This happens in such a repetitive cycle because the monetary issue is a consequence; it is the result of a major problem and not the primary cause of the ill situation. It is first and foremost an institutional affliction. It is and has been a misunderstanding of how our institutions should have been setup for proper growth and continuity of our evolution as a people.

It is important to understand that the only proven economic system that generates wealth and promotes freedom is the free enterprise of capitalism. An equine and its handler are only a winning mutual if the tracks and adequate rein are in place.

Therefore it is an exercise of evolutional progress that larger institutions come in, and aid smaller and technologically lacking countries. But, because the institutional model in existence is not extensive to 100% of the participants, it is imperative that we evolve to the institutional model of accessibility described in these notes. The lack of means of exchange that many experience is only a byproduct of wrong institutional behavior. Proper institutional performance will have appreciation for every possible multiplier effect in the economy: 100% of the participants.

Permanently eradicating disproportion is our only way out of the greater ills it provokes. There shouldn't exist polarity at all at the basic needs level. Nutrition, shelter, health and education must rise to the top in the list of priorities of every government in todays' world.

This World Bank type-institution would have a replica as representation in each and every one of the member countries it comes in negotiations with, unless the country in need of aid already has a Public Banking system. When negotiations are concluded then the bank is left behind becoming the national bank of said country.

This subsidiary is going to deal directly with the mining and or cultivation of the resources for international exchange. Every product being exported should be transacted through this world banking system.

Any one product manufactured for export that does not go through this banking system on its way out during the transport process is considered illegal trade. In this banking system any product that is banned from entering into any of the member countries would be listed in the network data base system of these institutions. Therefore the shipping of such products would be detained by the World Bank in the country of origin.

This World Bank or Public Banking Apparatus, should be considered the embassy of currency. The system would be interconnected for as long as the host nation is being assisted in creating financial independence. Any member country during such period of rehabilitation would know at all times how much of its national currency has legally entered into the banking system of other member countries.

Any one currency will be exchanged at the same rate everywhere in the world through the national World Bank. Any one country involved in international trade will automatically have this banking system setup before products leave its borders.

Having an eye on the movement of currency can deter misuse of the resources. Such caution does not mean that any one country would police or rule over another. Each country continues to operate its internal economy through its private banking system which doesn't have to be connected to the world banks outside its borders. We help our human brethren as often as possible and yet we should remain faithful to our own.

We are all similar in our basic human needs and the world is the one common place for us all. We all have different cultures and traditions; similar cultures should not become separated while exchanging our abundances for our lacks.

It is accurate to express that the banking institution is one of the key components and first appointee in collusion with the decentralization of government for resolving the imbalance at hand. Like the heart, the lungs, the spleen or the liver, the public ensemble of institutions must become that apparatus with activities within itself but not for itself.

It's only obvious that citizens of the deprived regions of the world will resolve towards a better haven. At first it's usually unnoticed until it becomes a critical situation. It will escalate. The situation must be fixed at origin and everyone will be happy at home. Even those that already migrated will want to return. No one is at a better place than at home in their country of origin. Jacob always longed his return to Israel.

No wonder England and the United States can exchange visitors without fear and in peace. The same with France and Spain. And even these powerful nations could do a better job towards their own citizens if the focus were on the welfare of every conceived and breathing human.

An institutional rehab must take place the world over. Developing and undeveloped nations must act at once, without delay. It's one easy but imperative task at hand. Unbelievable as it sounds, even the poorest of nations have fabricated extremely wealthy people among its ranks.

Those poor nations can't afford to diminish the few rich people remaining; with education and proper institutional arrangements, the wealth will reach everyone. In a very short time period they'll be rid of starvation, homelessness, illness and ignorance. That's one great per capita domestic yield.

Knowledge is a very noble reason for crossing borders. Students travel abroad for professional instruction. Certain schools are known for their academic programs and the achievement of their graduates. Many times these students arrive at the host country and bring their own wealth. Wealth that in many circumstances have been amassed by intelligently working parents.

In other situations these students are sponsored by institutions in their countries of origin and even governments. These are the guarantees desired when someone leaves their nation for another. Assurance that they will not become a burden to the host nation. Assurance that they will proudly accept being of a different culture, but not necessarily feeling a foreigner. Assurance that they will return home to continue enjoying in their own culture.

All of this is about to happen. All it takes is one nation with love for its own. Just like the first nomad to become settled and start a family; just like the next, and trading amongst themselves became the norm. Just the same as they maintained their common water stream and started their first institutions together.

Nations are comprised of many assets, people being the most important and indispensable of all. In the early marketplace associations its members were committed to sharing in the responsibility of maintaining their commonalities in the best shape and the most beneficial to all.

In that same link of ideas, those that made best use of their intellectual capabilities gained benefits according to their efforts. They amassed great wealth from a source that was common to all. Those people upon becoming the pillars of their communities, did the best to maintain their natural resources. They stayed in the knowing that one day their children, and their children's children, would need to find those natural resources as beneficial as they had found them.

Life has changed plenty since our ancestors first encountered it. Today we have an effective means of acquiring the products that the modern marketplace of today has to offer. We no longer go to the barbershop with a chicken to exchange it for a haircut.

Our marketplace today exchanges in currency. Europeans exchange in Euros, the Japanese in Yens; the Russians have their Ruble, Mexico has Pesos;

and every country takes care of domestic business transactions in their own currency.

When the economies shifted to the exchange of products and services for its currency estimated value, not every national owned currency to exchange for the upkeep of their most basic needs. The medical professionals no longer accepted to exchange their services for products or even other services. The economy was no longer run in such a fashion.

The economy had taken a great leap for the better. But, in the process of doing so, the most important factor in the equation was not taken adequately into consideration. A wonderful competition was on its way but all the participants were not equally suited at the start of the race.

The governments that created and still today regulate the currency business did not allocate the basic currency amounts necessary to make its per capita equally equipped in the fields of nutrition, shelter, health and education. Basic needs for an adequate functioning of the Intellectual Collective were not accounted for.

The institutional orchestra does not correspond to affording everyone with an equal threshold of opportunities. Such is an indispensable requirement for a State to pull away from the ranks of failure. Totally basic for a nation's success.

Can the State be both government and the basic needs provider for its people? There is no need to lie to ourselves in answering such questioning. Experience has proven that both are not possible to be achieved successfully. There lies the main reason for decentralizing government. Let's equip government with the ease of conducting policy and the people with the capability of providing for itself.

Establishments have grown disproportionally large pretending to look out for every citizen; we know that's not achievable. People need to be able to produce for themselves in their own communities.

The realities of the life that the citizens endure give proof that one large central government is incapable of providing for all. The people need to become empowered to be their own chaperons. Same reason being that accountants aren't allowed to write checks in an organized and successful enterprise. And besides, who wants to be a burden of the state? Where's the pride in that?

The basic needs of the people have to be met; period. Don't meet those, then you're a failed State; period. With this premise in mind, the public banking system is to be charged with holding, supervising and allocating currency to the private banking system. Private banking is to organize and carry out the financial transactions needed in the economy. Never should the public banking system extend funds to an end user.

A State Government should gather and administer information, facilitate and delegate when dealing with the matters pertaining to the Intellectual Collective within its confines.

The Banking Institution should see that the production of food is funded, and that sustainable farming is also capitalized. The industrialization of food should be promoted and financed aggressively. The climate funding the industrialization process should be one where the bank partners with the individual investors for a period of time. Such partnerships will only remain effective until the investments and substantial benefits have been restored to its vaults achieving success for the capitalists and the entrepreneurs.

Banks must remain profitable and investors must be able to stay in business for continuity of a healthy economy. The public banking system should serve as a registrar of the funds collected in the taxation endeavors. Never should public banking conduct transactions other than receiving from engravers and allocating to the private system.

Banks administer and have personnel supervising that housing is built affordably and efficiently. That the health Institutions receive the necessary funds when dispensing health to the Intellectual Collective. The Banking Institution is to foresee that an appropriate health industry is in place. The order is to manufacture the most qualifying equipment for proper health maintenance. Also promotion, adequate investment and provision of counseling. Adopting a responsible roll in the overall success of the industry is of the utmost importance.

Education being the integrator of all the basic needs should be appointed a committee of professional private citizens. A committee dedicated to the success of each individual student in a school. Such professionals will be charged with selecting the appropriate human teaching assets. The collegiate team will be having all the necessary equipment for building a curriculum that includes an essential practical knowledge in the arts, sciences, trades and sports.

Furthermore, a mastery in one of the above would be required of each student. A mastery in a combination of them would be a desirable achievement asked of each student. Prior to all this, the population of students would have been formerly considered in their tutors appropriation of funds. The census performing institutions will be the indispensable allied of the bankers in their job of funding every productive activity of the Collective.

Banks were created to preserve wealth. To keep it safe from ruffians. Banks are not to become ruffian institutions themselves. Nothing more shameful than banks repossessing people's assets and then putting them on the market for less than actual value.

Those are the actions that make the economy falter. Currency has a nominal value, but never value in itself. In order for it to acquire value it has to be materialized into goods and services. In the setting of an example, a fitting analogy: when a person purchases a ham and cheese sandwich they eat it and restore energy into the body; people cannot eat the monies used to purchase the sandwich and expect to restore value to the body.

Many will argue how then will the banking industry stay in business and make money to exchange for its expenses? Simply put, the banking institution will partner with and counsel its clients before and during the life of an investment. Every partner in a business operation stands to walking away with a profit. Not happening in today's economy because it simply isn't the custom yet. Banks will not be partners for the life of the business, only until a substantial benefit is achieved. Laws governing such relationship are to be promulgated in the scheme of things. Today's larger governments being so expensive require that taxes be overly hefty on the pockets of the investor. This model of productivity will reduce governments while increasing tax collection. Besides, in such a win-win situation, government will not be reminiscent of being large.

Governments have to start being less expensive. Banks have to be totally involved in the creation of wealth for the Intellectual Collective. The people should be empowered through selection of a small congress of private citizens overseeing the proper functioning of each of its institutions. Legislation has to be passed to validate the required overhaul necessary in each nation according to its needs.

The sentiment of patriotism, as it stands, is unilateral in most countries. The same as when the Roman Empire existed. It has not evolved much. Quoting JFK, "Ask not what your country can do for you, ask what you can do for your country". How many countries can still ask this of their citizens today?

We must ask with regards to all the people struggling in many countries, what can their governments do to remediate their plight? Continue with the impoverishment whip until they flee and become illegal immigrants of other nations?

Can each government vouch for its people abroad, morally and financially? If each government were required to go to bat for each of its citizens when abroad there would not exist much illegal migration. If the solution to the per capita needs were accessible as described herein for each citizen, the citizens of one nation would not be the burden of another.

How is it possible that the Intellectual Collective has to usually seek their welfare in other nations while their native government is ever larger? Isn't this a description of that which national pride is all about? How are those not failed states?

Even when the super powers don't align with the ideal World Bank scenario exposed herein, each individual nation can still remediate their embarrassing poverty situation. All it takes is the application of the methods we have described here, therefore meeting the per capita needs of its Intellectual Collective. It does take a concerted effort to take action, but the results will be immediately palpable. No need to procrastinate.

The world should be open to anyone wanting to travel for tourism if they can provide a clear background check. If the individual is traveling from an origin of known illegal migration, all it takes is the setting up of an escrow account. An account in their

CONCLUSION

You are highly appreciated. Your time and efforts are being well invested. Please spread the good news and educate us with your best comments.

MUCH LOVE.

Osiris Cabral

Osiriscabral10@gmail.com

Osiris Cabral on Instagram

Osiris Cabral on LinkedIn

Osiris Cabral on Facebook

name and in the name of the host nation. The bank account should contain enough money to provide for at least one month living expenses, medical insurance, and a travel insurance that would cover for return expenses in case the traveler defaults.

Aside from the escrow account, the traveler should purchase a round trip ticket. If the traveler isn't visiting a friend or relative that can set them up for their time abroad, then additional currency should be accounted for to make up for the cost of living through the intended sojourn.

A refillable bank card will be issued by the World Bank of the country of origin. If and when the balance is nearing a preset low limit of the escrow amount, automatic messages are to be sent to the travelers' smartphone. Provisions should be made so that in the case of losing access to said phone or bankcard, the traveler could present themselves to the nearest bank and have their information uploaded on a new phone. A smartphone will always pinpoint the location of its holder. Phone carriers will have to regulate who they are extending their services to. The escrow money should be immediately available for withdrawal upon arrival to origin.